MINIENCYCLOPEDIA
OF
WATER
GARDENING

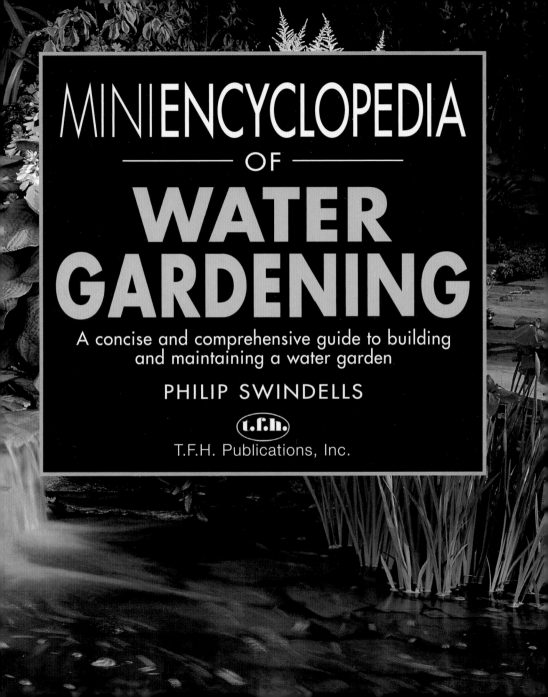

MINIENCYCLOPEDIA

— OF —

WATER GARDENING

A concise and comprehensive guide to building
and maintaining a water garden.

PHILIP SWINDELLS

t.f.h.

T.F.H. Publications, Inc.

Interpet Publishing

© 2004 Interpet Publishing Ltd.

Published 2004 by
T.F.H. Publications, Inc.
One TFH Plaza
Neptune City, NJ 07753
www.tfh.com

Library of Congress
Publication Data available upon
request.
ISBN 0-7938-0536-8

Editor: Philip de Ste. Croix
Designer: Philip Clucas MSIAD
Studio photography: Neil Sutherland
Artwork: Rod Ferring, Martin Reed,
    Stuart Watkinson
Production management: Consortium,
    Poslingford, Suffolk
Print production: DNA Printing
    Solutions, Ipswich
Printed and bound in China

CONTENTS

Introduction

O f all the different aspects of horticulture, water gardening must figure as one of the most fascinating. Within a pond there is another world, a complete eco-system in which the plants, fish and snails all depend upon one another. Managing such a finely balanced and complex environment is tremendously satisfying.

However, a pond is not the only form of water garden. Nowadays the use of water extends well beyond the pool, the bog garden and stream. There are self-contained fountains, bubbling millstones, wall masks and waterfalls. The tide of innovation that has spread through water gardening in recent years has made it one of the most popular forms of gardening.

Gardeners with a passion for plants can grow a unique range once water has been introduced to the garden. Beautiful waterlilies, with their often fragrant and always brightly colored blossoms floating serenely amongst verdant lily pads; stately iris in a rich and seemingly unending diversity of color; and swaying reeds and rushes; all become a possibility. In the water there are submerged plants busily working to maintain clear water and a balanced ecology, while above free-floating plants provide shelter from the summer sun for ornamental fish.

For those who have an interest in wildlife, the garden pond is a joy, not only providing a safe haven for aquatic life, but also serving as a stopping off place for birds and other creatures and coincidentally playing an important role in local wildlife conservation. Water gardening is truly a wonderful and rewarding pastime.

Left: *An enticingly lit curtain of water tumbles gracefully into a pool; it embodies the allure of the water garden that lies in wait for the imaginative gardener.*

WHAT ARE MY OPTIONS?

FORMAL FEATURES

*A*formal water feature should conform to certain criteria, irrespective of its size. Its design should be based upon sound mathematical principles and use lines, arcs and circles to establish a balanced outcome. At its simplest, a formal water feature is square, oblong, oval or circular. However, it can also be a linked complex of these elements, resulting in a pond that is elaborate, but still formal in character.

A formal water feature is most at ease in a formal garden landscape. Whether it be a small courtyard garden or sweeping lawn, the design principles are the same, the pond both reflecting and complementing the lines

Left and above: *Formality can take on a different appearance depending upon the materials that are used. Here each water feature emphasizes the particular feel and atmosphere of its garden setting.*

and shapes of the garden features around it. Often the pond becomes the major focus of the garden, and then adaptations and compromises are made to the surrounding garden landscape.

Formality tends to suggest severity and constraint, but the reality is very different. It offers liberation to the innovative water gardener, a freedom that those who embark upon an informal pond are often unable to enjoy. Raised and sunken ponds, linked water features and the use of both

conventional and outrageous modern materials are all permitted, the only constraint being that when plants and fish are to be part of the scheme, proper provision is made for them in the underwater pond profile.

Formal water gardening can be a great adventure. Aquatic plants and the pleasures

Above: *This beautiful and tranquil pool demonstrates how even a relatively austere design can be softened by its associated planting and the skillful use of ornament.*

of fishkeeping can be fully enjoyed, and the opportunity taken to exploit the qualities of both reflective and moving water to full effect.

INFORMAL FEATURES

Informal water features can be accommodated comfortably in all but the most formal and minimalist garden settings. There is a greater degree of flexibility regarding their placement in the garden landscape than is the case with a formal water feature, but an informal pond has many more constraints placed upon it with regard to its design and structure. Both aesthetically and practically it has to conform to a fairly constrained scheme.

The temptation to produce a pond structure with all manner of fussy niches and contortions should be resisted – in terms of both construction and management, these can be tiresome. In any event, many such features become hidden by plant growth. An informal pond should be designed in a series of sweeping arcs and curves, and this simplicity should also be reflected in any associated stream or waterfall feature.

Plants and ornamental fish are usually a high priority in an informal water feature. So it is important to consider the pond profile and to make appropriate accommodations

Below: *This pond focuses upon the waterfall, but it is brought to life by strong peripheral planting.*

Above and right: *Although informal ponds are planted generously with aquatic plants, it is important that they reveal sufficient open water to let you enjoy reflections.*

for them. Informal ponds are generally more diverse in character than in design, and apart from being decorative, many are now constructed very much with the conservation and enjoyment of wildlife in mind.

An informal pond is a watery canvas upon which the garden artist paints a picture with plants and fish. Yet it is also a complex world where all the living elements depend upon one another for their continued existence. It is a fascinating and busy place which will repay the pondkeeper with many hours of enjoyment.

THE MODERN STYLE

*A*lthough home water gardening is a fairly recent innovation, unlike most other aspects of gardening it has experienced rapid change, especially during the past decade. Television gardening programs have had an obsession with water features, and improvements in modern technology have greatly simplified pond construction and maintenance. This tremendous surge of interest has brought with it all kinds of innovations and a corresponding richness of styles and fashions.

Metal, glass and plastics are now much in vogue, especially for moving water features. Lighting has also become very sophisticated and can transform a water garden into a glittering evening wonderland at the touch of a button. The age of the computer has ushered in remote-controlled

Above: *Modern technology has created all manner of possibilities for innovation in the water garden. Many modern materials are ideal for the inventive gardener.*

moving water features, and introduced both dancing and musical fountains. Indeed, almost anything is possible in the modern water garden.

Plants are continually being improved, enormous strides having being made in recent years with the development of hardy waterlilies. Marginal aquatics, through

Above: *Minimalist lines and strong blocks of color turn this pebble fountain into a design statement.*

careful selection, have made great advances too, and new hybrids of plants hitherto unknown to pond owners have brought myriad new plant association and design possibilities.

All of this is very exciting for the water gardener, but a word of caution should be sounded. Often these exciting innovations are launched at major flower shows where they are displayed to their best advantage. However, a flower show is much akin to a theater. Before stepping into the unknown, fully assess the materials and equipment being shown to determine whether they are likely to fulfill the role intended in the practical garden.

CONTAINER FEATURES

*I*t is not necessary to have a pond to enjoy the many pleasures of water gardening. Container water features can offer as much diversity as a garden pond, for not only are there many pygmy waterlilies and dwarf aquatic plants available with which to stock them, but also a range of miniaturized pumps and attachments that enable the imaginative gardener to enjoy a tiny fountain or cascade within the confines of a large pot on the patio or balcony.

Most container water gardens are created in pots, bowls or troughs, although any vessel that holds water has the potential to be transformed into a water feature. Everything from a sink to a watering can may be used and will potentially give endless enjoyment to its owner.

Nowadays it is possible to visit the local garden center and see an array of containers with submersible pumps, ready for you simply

Below: *The development of the modern submersible pump has enabled self-contained water features to become more sophisticated than ever. Options include modern metallic designs like this waterlily fountain.*

to add water and plug into the electricity supply. These range from half barrels with old fashioned hand pumps attached, and through which the water flow is powered by a submersible pump, to hand-crafted copper leaf cascades, and bubbling spheres that rotate while water glides over them continuously.

Although small, such container water features demand regular attention, especially with regard to replenishing water lost to evaporation. Small planted containers also require care, for with such a tiny body of water it is impossible to maintain a natural ecological balance as with a pond. Thus water changing is a regular requirement.

Right: *This bubbling pot fountain sits over a small reservoir containing the pump. Water trickles down the sides and is returned to the reservoir through the cobbles that surround it.*

DECORATIVE FEATURES

While a pond is the main focus of a water garden, there are many additional features that can be added which enhance its appearance and tie it more intimately to the surrounding garden. While care should be taken not to interfere with planting opportunities, nor to obscure the reflective qualities of the water, much can be done to improve both the visual appeal of the water garden and its practicality.

The most useful improvements pertain to the edges where the pond meets dry land. This area is often an unresolved nightmare, and so planting scrambling plants as a disguise is the usual outcome. It is a reasonable solution, but the use of decorative paving or the creation of a cobble beach is a more practical and visually appealing answer.

Decking offers a further option, for not only can this tidy up the pond edge, but it also provides an additional recreational or sitting area. Sometimes it can extend into the pond, rather like a small landing stage, or even extend as a causeway. However, when the water is to be crossed, then a bridge or stepping stones provide the answer. Indeed, a bridge is usually an impressive focal point, as well as a practical addition.

Garden lighting has become very popular in recent times and never more so than with the water garden. There are wonderful opportunities for up-lighting, mirroring and silhouetting. Fountains, waterfalls and wall masks can all be simply illuminated with a range of techniques that quickly transform them into objects of great beauty.

Left: *In the modern water garden the focal point need not always be a fountain. Sculpture and abstract art can also be comfortably included.*

Above: *Subtle plant arrangements that either frame or provide a background to pond ornamentation, such as this impressive glass centerpiece, can make an enormous difference on its impact.*

Left: *A fine example of how bright metal and flowing water can combine to produce a fountain that is sculptural in effect. The simple raised pool is a perfect visual complement.*

PLANNING
& BUILDING

Basic Principles of Water Garden Construction

The most critical factor to take into account when establishing a water garden is siting. Ideally, a garden pool, or other water feature where plants are to figure prominently, should be constructed in a position of full and uninterrupted sunlight. For a viable eco-system to establish, lusty plant growth is essential and all aquatic plants must have plenty of light.

Visually, water is always more appealing when situated at the lowest point in the landscape. This cannot always be arranged, but when it can, take care to see that the site is not waterlogged and that the water table does not rise dramatically during the winter. A water table close to the surface of the soil can cause unwanted ballooning of a pool liner.

It is also essential to know where services to the house or other buildings are laid. It is extremely frustrating to be close to completing an excavation and coming unexpectedly across a water or gas main. Any use of electricity should strictly follow regulatory advice and all equipment must be specifically manufactured for use with water. Nowadays there is a wide range of pumps, lights and other electrical equipment available which comply with strict codes of practice.

Above: *This pond illustrates the problems of building on a slope. Because levels were not properly checked during excavation, the pool is not level. The liner is exposed on the right while water laps the rim on the left.*

Above: *Underground service pipes and cables can create difficulties during pool construction, especially when they are come upon during excavation. Check where pipes run while planning the pool.*

Below and below left: *These are not good sites for a pool. A low area, which collects water, can cause problems during the winter, the pressure of ground water ballooning a pool liner or lifting a pre-formed pool out of the ground. Tree roots can cause similar problems, and shade and fallen leaves are undesirable.*

CHECK LIST

- Situate the water feature in full sun.
- Keep away from overhanging trees because of falling leaves and disruptive roots.
- Keep away from trees of the cherry family, the winter host of the waterlily aphid.
- Check the location of existing underground services to avoid damaging them during excavation.
- Prepare the site for installation of required underground services, e.g. electricity.
- Visually, water is best placed at the lowest point in the landscape, but avoid waterlogged areas.
- Ensure that the site does not flood. Install a drain if necessary.
- Ensure the provision of suitable depths of water for both deep-water and marginal aquatics.
- Make any preparations necessary to ensure that safety measures can be made to keep children safe.

The Right Materials

There are many different methods available for constructing water features. A wide array of man-made linings—from pvc and polythene to rubber and bentonite matting—have revolutionized pond construction. Pre-formed ponds of fibreglass, plastic or composition materials offer another simple method of creating a water garden, although these do not give quite the flexibility of design allowed by pond liners.

Pond liners are used to line an excavation that is in the shape of the final pond. In many cases pond liners are vulnerable to damage, especially in stony soil, and so an underlay has to be provided. This is usually in the form of a specially manufactured fabric fleece.

Streams are most effectively created with a liner, for they can be more imaginatively designed and the levels better controlled than by the use of pre-formed sections that clip together. Twists and turns in the stream bed are also more easily accommodated when working with flexible liner.

The same applies with waterfall and cascade units. When pre-formed, they have the advantage of being watertight, quick to use and producing a consistent spread and flow of water, but the materials from which they are made often have a rather artificial appearance.

Above: *There are a wide variety of pre-formed pools available in a selection of materials. All are very durable and not difficult to install. Make sure that the marginal shelves are sufficiently large to accommodate planting baskets.*

Above: *Pre-formed cascade units are easily installed and rarely present any problems with water seepage around the edges. However, they are more difficult to disguise with planting than liner.*

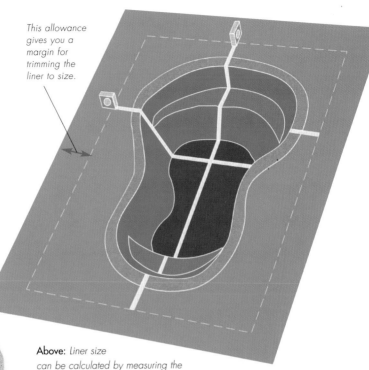

This allowance gives you a margin for trimming the liner to size.

Above and below: *Irregular shapes can be drawn by sprinkling sand freehand.*

Above: *Liner size can be calculated by measuring the pool, embracing the depth and any shelves, at the widest and longest points. These figures give the maximum width and length of the liner required. Allow a margin for an overlap all round.*

Right: *This is a neat way of marking out the shape of an oval excavation. An inverted soft drink bottle is filled with dry sand. The string, which is anchored around two pegs, is pulled taut and a sand line is used to inscribe the oval.*

Selecting The Right Components For the Job

The gardener who wishes to extend a water feature, perhaps by creating a waterfall or fountain, has many options. It is not necessary to put together a complex proposal, for at the garden center all manner of exciting opportunities await the enthusiast. Pre-formed waterfalls and cascade units take so much of the work out of creating such a feature. Not only are they guaranteed to be watertight, but they are of such a configuration that when the pump is switched off, some water remains lying in the units.

There are a whole range of readymade fountains which comprise an ornament and a pump which just need placing in the pool and switching on. Some are tiny and can be used in pot or container arrangements, while others are gushing jets in the best traditions of classical designs and require a generous spread of water.

Modern interchangeable hoses, connectors, valves and couplings all provide instant watertight connections which enable the water gardener to put together innovative designs if the package or kit is not appealing. No longer are soldering and brazing essential skills for constructing exciting and unusual creations. A spanner and screwdriver are usually all that is required.

Above and below: *There is a wide range of pipes and easily installed pipe fittings available off the shelf at the garden center or DIY store. These make the production of quite elaborate arrangements simple, even for the beginner. The most versatile and durable pipe is ridged like a vacuum cleaner hose.*

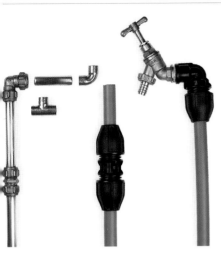

POOL LINERS

A pool liner is a good option for creating a pond, waterfall or stream. Special felt underlay is used to cushion and protect the liner from any protruding sharp stones in the soil.

Pipework can be joined by using special metal or plastic connector pieces. Another invaluable item is the screw-up jubilee clip (right).

Below: Pre-formed pools are of the right shape and configuration for successfully creating pleasing water flows. They are also guaranteed to be watertight.

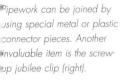

Pre-formed waterfall and stream units are convenient and easy to use, but they do not weather as attractively as natural materials do.

Pumps and Filters

There are two main kinds of pumps: submersible and surface. For most gardeners, the surface kinds are now of little relevance, for they are only employed to displace very large volumes of water and are rarely necessary in a domestic situation. Submersible pumps are available in a wide variety and can fulfill most of the requirements of the average pond owner. There are also miniature pumps which can yield a modest flow compatible with the tiniest container feature.

Filters are also useful adjuncts to a pump, especially in a pool where there is no prospect of natural balance, as is usually the case where moving water dominates. There are three main filtration systems. The mechanical kind physically removes suspended particles and debris by passing water through a filter medium. Biological filters depend on the action of bacteria to digest waste products in the water (see also page 198), while UV filters use ultra-violet light to kill algae and other micro-organisms.

With a pump the most important factor is the flow rate: the amount of water that the pump displaces per minute or hour. A simple test to calculate the necessary capacity involves measuring the desired water flow for one minute, converting it into gallons or liters, and multiplying the figure by 60 to give a flow rate per hour.

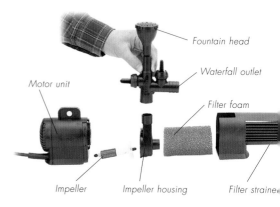

Motor unit — *Fountain head* — *Waterfall outlet* — *Filter foam* — *Impeller* — *Impeller housing* — *Filter strainer*

Above: *The component parts of a modern submersible pump showing the power unit, impeller, impeller housing, fountain jet with dual output to both fountain head and waterfall, filter foam, and the filter strainer.*

Above: *Before purchasing a pump to run a waterfall it is important to ensure that the water flow rate is right. The figure can be established by running a hosepipe into the cascade unit at a rate that satisfies you and measuring the water flowing over it for the period of a minute.*

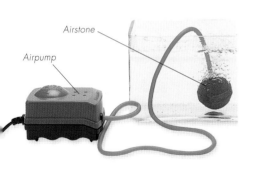

Airstone

Airpump

Above: This pump does not move water, but it distributes air into the water and is intended as a means of oxygenating a pool where there is a large population of fish.

Above right: The ultra-violet filter is effective against all algae. Water that is laden with suspended algae returns to the pond clear. UV filtration is the most reliable method of ensuring clear water where a natural balance is impossible to establish.

Filter brushes

Left: This is a multi-brush filter unit. The filter brushes take out most of the suspended material. The additional filter medium then works both mechanically and biologically. Colonies of bacteria grow on the medium and they convert fish waste in harmless by-products.

Outlet pipe

Sponge filter

The filter body contains the filter medium. Water enters from below and exits from the top outlet.

Ceramic filter medium

Biological filter medium

Right: A compact filter which may be used both in and out of a pool. It operates using a ceramic filter medium. This is placed in the bottom and a thick filter sponge is added. The lid and outlet pipe is then attached. Filters like this help to maintain water clarity.

Your First Steps

When establishing a pond, it is important to consider the site very carefully. Certain factors will affect the pond visually and they are very personal in their nature, but there are others that affect the way in which the pond functions practically, and they should be carefully heeded.

The most important factor is sunlight. A pond must be positioned in full uninterrupted sunlight if the plants and fish are to prosper. Sunlight is equally important for a pool consisting of just open water and where plants are not required, for it is the play of light with its varied reflections upon the water that gives such a feature its appeal. If the pond is being constructed during the winter time, observe nearby deciduous trees, for these may cast shadows in unexpected areas during the summer when they are in full leaf. The falling leaves from trees are also a nuisance during the autumn. So overhanging branches must be avoided. Many trees have invasive roots, those of willows and poplar being particularly disruptive. When in close proximity to a pond, they can cause heaving and fracturing of the liner.

The site for a pond must also be well-drained. Ironically, a permanently wet area may not be a good position for a pond, as the pressure of a high water table can dislodge a pre-formed structure, literally forcing it out of the soil, and also cause the ballooning of a liner.

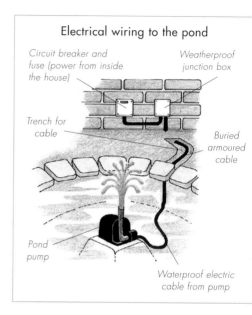

Electrical wiring to the pond

Circuit breaker and fuse (power from inside the house)

Weatherproof junction box

Trench for cable

Buried armoured cable

Pond pump

Waterproof electric cable from pump

It is essential when laying an electrical cable to a water feature to ensure that it is covered adequately with soil in a deep trench, and that it is manufactured for outdoor use. An armoured cable (as shown above) is to be preferred.

Above: *When considering the placement of a water feature, it is important to mark out the area taking into account local features such as the shade cast by trees and the incline of the land.*

Above: *It is important to get the shape of a pool and stream right before the first turf is cut. Mark out the shape on the ground with hose or rope. Check that everything works visually, and also practically with regard to the lie of the land.*

– LAYING AN ELECTRIC CABLE

2 To protect a buried cable from accidental excavation damage, cover it with a layer of sand and lay a course of tiles across the top. The chances of the cable being disturbed by a thrusting spade are remote.

3 Once the tiles are installed, stick a hazard tape on them. These tapes are weather- and rot-proof and give an early warning of impending danger if digging or other earthmoving activities take place in the immediate vicinity.

Marking Out The Site

Having selected a suitable site, the first task is to mark out the position of the pool accurately. For a liner pool this can be done with a series of strings, pegs and simple mathematical formulae which most of us learned at school.

Apart from ensuring accuracy of form, it is important to get the pool level. Even a small deviation can cause both water spillage on one side and exposure of the inner pool-side on the other. Position a mean level peg and then work from this with a board and level, ensuring that the whole area is accurately assessed. Soil can then be redistributed according to the various levels indicated by the pegs. When installing a liner it is preferable to take the lowest point in the levelling process and to transfer the mean level peg to that position.

With a pre-formed pool, accurate levelling is just as vital. While there are recommendations which suggest that an excavation can be accurately created to accommodate the shelves of a pre-formed pool, it is generally preferable to dig a hole that embraces the maximum length, breadth and depths of the pool and to position it within the all-embracing hole. Backfilling to fill in any voids in the soil once the pre-formed pool is in place is usually easiest with pea-gravel.

1 You must establish the levels of the ground where the pool is to be dug. Set a datum peg to the desired level, and use more pegs and a spirit level to accurately establish the horizontal.

FORMING A RIGHT ANGLE

A right angle can be created by marking out a triangle using Pythagoras' 3-4-5 system of measurement.

2 Measure the distance to the ground of your first datum peg. This is the level at which you want all the edges of the pool to sit when the plot has been excavated.

3 Now transfer this measurement to the other pegs in all directions across the site. This shows where the soil needs cutting away or filling up to establish a flat surround.

MAKING A CIRCLE

1 Place a peg in the center of the intended circle. Attach a string and use a second cane to inscribe the circumference.

2 Use sand to distinguish the score mark clearly in the turf. It also gives a good impression of how the finished pool will fit into the garden plan.

THE FORMAL OPTION

A formal pool is constructed on mathematical principles, normally being a square, rectangle, circle or arc, or a combination of these configurations, which fit comfortably into a formal garden landscape. While plants and fish are usually regarded as important, they need not be part of a formal scheme, for such a pool can be created merely for the reflective quality of the water that it contains, or as a setting for a fountain or other moving water spectacle.

Without aquatic plants, the prospects for a healthy watery environment are poor and so a filtration system must be considered.

There are many of these to choose from, but for the most part they comprise either a biological or chemical system with the option of UV filtration as an addition. Modern filters are very effective, easy to install and manage, and operate simply with a submersible pump. If carefully planned from the outset, they can be comfortably accommodated into the water feature design without visual intrusion.

Below: *Bold plantings arranged strategically around the pond provide color, soften the edges, and yet do not interfere with the overall formality of the feature.*

A circular pool lends itself well to a fountain and can also be used effectively at the end of a path where a hedge or wall forms a background. In many ways an oval pool is more versatile visually than a circular one because it can create an illusion of greater length or breadth depending upon its orientation.

The appearance of a garden can be greatly altered by the shape of the pool. A narrow pool across the garden gives a widening effect, while lengthways it suggests a longer garden. A narrowing pond can give the illusion of a distant perspective.

Above: *With formal designs you must maintain a balance between shapes and sizes; here, both are in harmony.*

Below: *Formality on different levels – raising this circular pool uses a small space to maximum advantage.*

As well as the traditional sunken formal pool, there are opportunities for creating raised water features. Visually, it is only possible to defy nature and lift water above the surrounding landscape with a formal feature. Raised ponds need not be large structures. There are some very attractive small self-assembly patio pools with the potential for both tasteful planting and the incorporation of moving water. These compact formal water features are extremely useful, not only for confined spaces but also as focal points in larger garden designs.

PROJECT: A Round Lined Pool

Marking out is achieved simply by using the two stakes and string method – a central stake has a string attached which is the radius of the pool, and attached to the end of this is a sharpened stake which scores out the position of the pool edge as it is scribed round the central peg in a circle. A trickle of sand can be used to delineate the outline more clearly if necessary. The depth and shelving arrangements should then be calculated and a quantity of liner purchased based upon the maximum length and breadth of the finished pool (measurements which are of course identical for a circular pool) plus twice the maximum depth.

The site must be made level or else there will be water spillage from the pool at one point and liner exposure at the opposite side. It is much simpler to prepare for this before digging begins than to try to rectify it when the liner has been laid and water added. The excavation should also ideally be created in undisturbed soil so that it can be carved out without minor soil movements. Thus, it is always preferable when levelling the site to reduce a higher area rather than to add soil to a low-lying part.

1 Mark out a circle on the ground using two pegs and a piece of string which is the length of the radius of the finished pool.

2 Remove the turf to produce the outline of the pool. Use a sharp spade or a turfing iron to make a neat job of the excavation.

3 It is important that the excavation is level as this will provide the overall pool profile. Check with a board and level regularly.

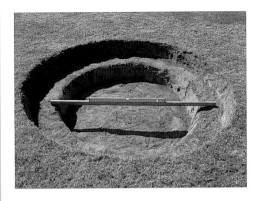

4 Ensure that the marginal shelves are level in each direction and are dug to the correct depth.

5 Check the hole and remove any sharp stones, twigs or other objects which may pierce the liner under the weight of water.

6 As an added precaution to guard against puncture, a layer of sand can be spread over the base of the excavation and the shelves.

PROJECT: A Round Lined Pool

The excavation is made to precisely the dimensions of the intended final pool, any sharp stones or other debris being carefully removed and protective pool underlay fabric installed. Damp bricklayers' sand can also be used to form a protective cushion, but this is not so useful where there are significant steep sides to cater for.

The liner should be spread out to warm in the summer sun before being introduced to the excavated hole. This makes it much more malleable and eases the problem of making neat folds when the time comes to do this. Water is then added and the liner begins to stretch to fit itself to the excavation. At this stage creases should be smoothed away as far as possible and the folds in the liner made to help it conform to the shape of the hole. Once the water has reached the top, the liner edge can be trimmed so that it can be disguised beneath paving or whatever edging is intended. Curved paving slabs make a sympathetic edging for this style of pool – they should be bedded onto mortar as illustrated.

 When working inside the empty pool, remember to slip your shoes off. The last thing you want is to pierce a hole in the liner.

7 The completed excavation is carefully lined with the pond liner underlay. Water it to help it conform to the shape of the hole.

10 Paving slabs provide the best formal edging. Allow a small overhang to produce a neat edge and remove any surplus liner.

8 The pool liner is placed as accurately as possible within the hole. Large regular folds are then made to eliminate creases.

9 Water is added. As the water rises, the folds can be adjusted and any small creases or wrinkles in the liner smoothed out.

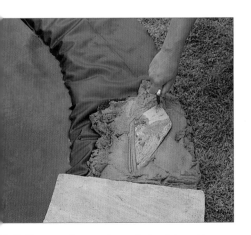

11 Excavate the area beneath the slab and liner and fill back to ground level with mortar. Poolside paving must be very secure.

12 Lay the slabs and ensure that they are level in every direction. Point the gaps between them evenly with mortar.

PROJECT: Fitting An External Filter

External filters permit the regular treatment of pond water and produce excellent results. Most extract solid debris and also pass the water through bio-blocks or similar material where aerobic bacteria convert toxic ammonia into nitrites and ultimately nitrates (see page 198).

External filters can be positioned on the surface of the ground next to the pool and discreetly hidden by vegetation. However, it is neater to sink them into the ground, accommodation often being made for them in a purpose-built chamber near the summit of a waterfall.

Once the filter box has been positioned, the lid can be replaced and the hole backfilled, taking care not to disturb the box. When a UV filter is included to kill algae in the water, this can be accommodated next to the main filter box.

The bio-filter and UV filter can then be connected and the pump attached to the filter feed hose. Once the pump is turned on, the filtration process begins. It will take four to six weeks in warm weather before the biological part of the filter establishes sufficient beneficial bacteria for the process of breaking down the harmful toxins in the water to get underway and the pond chemistry starts to improve.

1 First excavate the area where you want to sink the filter chamber into the ground.

2 Use a paving slab or a layer of bricks to provide a firm and level base for the filter.

3 Put the filter chamber in position. Ensure that it is level and secure before backfilling.

4 Replace the lid and backfill around the sides using either soil or fine pea gravel.

5 If the filter has a UV option, attach this close to the main filter so it is easily accessible when required. With the UV attachment in place, run the filter feed hose into the pool.

6 The pump is then attached to the filter. Make sure that the pump is powerful enough to operate the filter effectively.

7 Run the pump to make sure that it works properly. The biological filter will take several weeks to become fully effective.

8 It is a good idea to position some plants around the filter that will grow up and hide it from view. Once the filter is working efficiently, water clarity in the pool can almost be assured.

PROJECT: A Raised Pool

There are many options for building a raised pool, ranging from a standard brick or stone wall construction to a timber sleeper arrangement. It is possible to use an existing watertight vessel, such as a header tank, and build around it, or the feature may be created from scratch. For the inventive gardener, the latter option is to be preferred, for then the pool can be exactly what is required rather than the inevitable compromise offered by a container disguised by a surrounding wall.

As with pools that are sunk in the ground, it is important to have a level base from which to work with a raised pool. Remember that the underlying level of the ground is transferred upwards with a raised pool, and the problems of spillage and liner exposure are potentially the same as for an excavated pool.

Of all the construction materials that are available, properly preserved timber is the most versatile and also the most resistant to severe winter weather. Installing a liner is very easy in a timber pool, for it can be readily secured to the internal wooden walls using a narrow batten to trap the liner, which is then secured with roofing nails.

Above: *The completed pool. Architectural plants like bulrush and pickerel have been used to add a strong vertical note to the feature.*

1 Place the sleeper timbers in a square arrangement. Ensure that each one overlaps the junction between the timbers below it.

2 Secure the timbers in place with strong metal strips or ties. Use self-tapping screws and an electric screwdriver.

3 Measure the pool liner and fit it accurately into the structure, making bold folds in the corners to minimize creasing.

4 Using a staple gun, secure the liner to the wooden structure. Position the staples near the top edge of the liner.

5 Align the timber batten with the top edge of the timber structure so as to trap the liner in place. Secure it with roofing nails.

Aquatic compost is used to fill the planting area.

6 Create a marginal planting pocket by putting a square of liner underlay in a corner, and build a box-like structure with loose bricks.

7 Once the container area has been completed, add good garden soil or aquatic planting compost. Plant into this and top dress with pea gravel.

PROJECT: A Patio Pool

There are many opportunities for creating a small water feature on a patio. It is mostly undesirable to excavate a pool in such a position, as the soil is unlikely to be compacted and stable, a prerequisite when using a liner. Apart from such vagaries of construction, a sunken pool in a patio will gather all sorts of leaves and debris that blow into it. A raised pool not only alleviates all these practical

problems, but offers the gardener the opportunity to enjoy the beauty of the plants and activities of the fish closer to hand. Raised pools available to the home gardener are generally of simple construction, but they are very effective. They consist either of a rigid container around which an outer decorative surround is built, or are of a modular construction, usually of timber, which is lined with a pool liner which is secured internally with wooden battens or carpet strip. While the majority depend upon a conventional lining, there are now constructions in which the pool liner is pre-formed and welded into a shape which drops into the structure where it fits exactly, without any need for folds or tucks.

1 The pre-formed timber sections are already treated with a preservative, but are visually bland and uninteresting. Garden stains or wood paints help brighten their appearance.

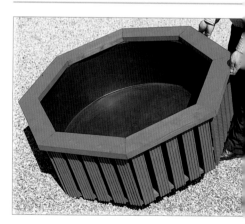

4 Once the whole pool structure is complete, it can be positioned. It is important to have a level situation, such as a terrace, on which to site it permanently.

2 Small metal fasteners are screwed into the main bearers, both at the top and the bottom. These provide the structure with rigidity. It is important that they are accurately installed.

3 When most of the sections have been screwed together, the tub which forms the pool is slid into the prepared framework. The final fixings are then made.

5 Fill the pool with water. It looks best if the final level in such a pool is established just a couple of centimeters beneath the overhang of the top surround. If a pump is to be installed, create a small level plinth with a few loose housebricks.

6 Position the pump centrally and ensure that the top of the fountain nozzle is just above the water surface. Take care to hide the electrical cable as neatly as possible. Switch the pump on and adjust the spray height to suit the space.

A MIRROR TO NATURE

Most gardeners hanker for a natural water feature. They dream of an open body of water that has been fashioned by nature and is therefore in complete harmony with its surroundings. It should be pleasing to the eye and only require enhancing by tasteful planting. However, for most gardeners the reality is that a pond has to be artificially contrived and introduced to the existing garden landscape.

The success of this is largely determined by the plants and features that bind it to its surroundings. Although a rock feature combining a waterfall is a frequent accompaniment to a natural water feature, a bog garden also provides an excellent means of linking the pond to the garden. At the same time it provides an opportunity for extended planting, which is especially useful with a wildlife pond. It is preferable to establish a bog garden at the same time as the pond is constructed. It is then easier to decide upon scale and proportions and to create them as a single entity.

Another essential in achieving success with a natural water feature is the thoughtful use of construction materials. It is generally inappropriate to lay concrete or paving in close proximity to the pond, since these, unless very cleverly integrated, tend to spoil the natural effect. Where hard landscaping materials are desired, then natural stone should be used. A carefully considered planting scheme also contributes greatly to the success of a natural water feature, the arrangement of plants growing in an unrestricted fashion providing much of its desired informality.

Left: *In addition to the water itself, tasteful and generous peripheral planting contributes greatly to a pond's attractiveness to wildlife.*

Tips & handy hints

Natural bodies of water rarely have constrictions or acute angles. Water erodes the banks and produces contours that are smooth and gentle. Steep sides only occur naturally in association with rock formations. So when setting out to design a natural water feature all these aspects should be taken into consideration. Do not be tempted to create fussy niches and contortions.

The best effects in a bog garden are achieved by planting plants in groups. Treat a boggy area rather like an herbaceous border and group the plants in relation to their heights and colors.

Usually water only occurs naturally at the lowest point in the landscape. Try to recreate the same illusion when constructing a pond in the garden; it will inexplicably enhance its overall aspect.

Left: *A wonderful interpretation of nature that is visually appealing as well as being practical and functional. The pebble beach provides easy access to the water for birds, mammals and amphibians.*

PROJECT: An Informal Rigid Pond

Rigid ponds are very convenient for water garden construction, for all the levels are pre-determined and the pond shell is watertight. However, as with all ponds, a little thought is necessary before installation, especially with regard to the lie of the land. It is imperative that when the pond is in its final position that it is level from side to side and end to end.

Once this is achieved, the excavation can be created to suit the shape and size of the pond. Do not try to make it exactly the same size, but allow a little leeway so that when the pool is placed in position, small adjustments can be made. This also means that there is room to introduce a cushioning layer of sand and adequate space for backfilling.

When the pool has been positioned correctly and backfilled with sand, check one more time that the levels are correct. The paved edging can then be added. A shallow excavation will be necessary around the edge of the pond to accommodate the thickness of the paving and a shallow mortar bed in which to set it in order to make it secure. This will ensure that the edging and the surrounding grass are level.

 The edges of pre-formed pools tend to be quite unattractive. However, if a paved edge is allowed to overhang the water slightly, the edges of the pool can be easily disguised.

1 Spread sand carefully and accurately around the base of the pool to mark out the shape. Remove the pool shell before digging commences. Excavate to the depth of the marginal shelves.

4 Carefully lower the pool shell into the excavation. Make sure that it is sitting evenly on the sand bed.

48

2 Place the pond in the hole and mark around the outer edge with sand. Excavate the entire area. Remove an extra 5 cm (2 in) of soil to allow for a sand base and space for backfill.

3 Remove any sharp stones from the hole. Then cover the shelves with a 5 cm (2 in) layer of

5 With the pool in position, take a board and spirit level and adjust the pool as necessary to ensure that it is level from side to side and end to end.

6 Backfill with sand or washed pea shingle. This will flow evenly around the shell and support it securely.

PROJECT: Installing A Pump and Filter

When installing any filter other than a straightforward multi-purpose filter that sits within the pond, it is sensible to accommodate it separately to the side of the pond. The more complex filters, such as those that are both bio-filter and UV filter which will require regular supervision and maintenance, can be best managed in a

separate chamber and connected to the pump that operates within the pond.

Take care to ensure that the pump is powerful enough to operate the filter and any feature where water is to be moved. It is always wise to purchase a pump that has 25 percent more capacity than is required. It can always be controlled downwards.

Situate the pump within the pond either on the flat bottom or on a suitable plinth. It is important that the pump is level and stable and that it can be easily retrieved from the side of the pond for cleaning and maintenance on a regular basis. In the set-up illustrated here, the outfall side of the pump discharges clean water back into the pond through a decorative fountain, while the input element draws dirty water through the pump to the combined bio-filter and UV sterilizer system.

1 Assemble the fountain head and T-piece. Connect the hose using the largest diameter flexible hose that will fit the pump.

Above: *The bio-filter can be accommodated in a concrete collar situated beneath the paving at the poolside.*

2 Tighten up the hose clip so that it does not slip. Do not over-tighten, as the fountain-head connection may crack.

3 Push the T-piece onto the pump outlet. An extension tube can be fitted to lift the fountain head to the desired height.

4 The fountain regulator valve controls the water flow to the filter. As the fountain flow is increased, the filter flow lessens.

5 Position the pump in the pond before connecting it to the electricity supply. Connect the hose running from the pump to the inlet on the filter.

6 The return pipe taking water from the filter to the pond can be disguised by connecting it to an ornament, here a decorative fish. The pipes can be hidden away beneath the paving slabs. Once the water is running, check that the flow rate through the filter is sufficient for correct functioning. To work out the flow rate, time how long it takes to fill a 10-liter (2.6-gallon) bucket.

PROJECT: A Lined Informal Pool

Creating the shape of the pool is best achieved by using a length of hosepipe or rope to delineate its outline. This allows you to assess the overall look and proportion of the pool before you start to dig. Fussy corners are generally not desirable, as they present difficulties when it comes to putting in the liner and producing a crease-free finish.

A lined pool takes the shape of the final excavation. So shelves and levels are created solely from the soil profile. Thus, undisturbed ground is ideal for pool excavation. Previously cultivated soil can present difficulties and the collapsing of the pool profile can easily occur.

Stones can also be troublesome in a clay or loam soil, especially if they are near the surface, for water pressure within the liner can sometimes lead to puncturing as the stones are forced into the liner. To avoid this, an underlay should be used. It is put into the excavation and dampened so that it clings to the walls. The liner is then spread over this and the pool filled with water. As water is added, the liner should be smoothed out by hand. Creases are best removed as the pool fills, as they are impossible to deal with later.

1 Mark out the area of the intended excavation with a length of hosepipe. Ensure that the curves are smooth.

2 Excavate the pool to the depth of the shelves. The should be deep enough t take a planting basket.

3 Excavate the full depth of the pool, digging down from the marginal shelves to make the deepest area.

4 Level off the floor of the hole. Remove any stones or other sharp objects that may pierce the liner.

5 Ensure that the marginal shelves, as well as the edges of the pool, are level from side to side.

6 Place protective underlay into the excavation, moulding it to the shape of the hole.

7 Dampen the underlay and try to mould the liner to the contours of the hole. Make sure to allow sufficient overlap.

8 Remove as many creases as possible, working from the bottom up. It helps if the liner has been warmed by the sun.

9 Add water from a hosepipe. As the water rises and presses against the walls of the pool, smooth out the creases.

10 The pool is complete and ready for planting. The liner has been trimmed to shape and tucked under the grass at the edge of the pool. The stones placed around the edge help to hide the top of the pool liner from view along the margin of the shelves.

PROJECT: A Bog Garden

A bog garden can either be an integral part of the water garden or an independent feature in its own right. When sited adjacent to a pond, it is quite simple to use the water in the pond to maintain a suitable level of moisture in the soil by creating a permeable membrane between the two. If the bog garden is to be completely independent, then other arrangements have to be made to ensure constant moisture.

The construction of a bog garden is similar to that of a lined pool, except that there are no variable depths and the overall excavation need be no more than 45 cm (18 in). Thus, it is a shallow basin that is lined either with a pool liner or plain builders' polythene. As the lining is completely disguised and there is no direct contact with sunlight which can degrade polythene, any cheap waterproof material can be used.

Once the liner is installed, the base should be pricked with a fork to allow excess water to drain away during winter. A layer of gravel is added so that the holes will not become sealed by the heavy organic soil that bog garden plants so enjoy. An irrigation hose may also be introduced to ensure plentiful moisture.

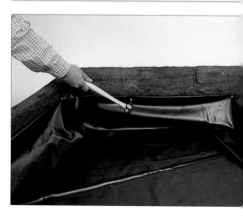

Above: *An attractively planted bog garden with a rich diversity of colorful, moisture-loving plants. Foliage color and form are an added bonus throughout the season.*

1 Here, the liner for the bog garden is being tacked to a timber frame with roofing nails.

2 With the liner in place, a fork is used to puncture it to provide some drainage holes.

3 A generous layer of gravel is raked over the floor of the bog garden to assist drainage.

4 Irrigation hose is put in place so that, when complete, the moisture level can be controlled.

A wide range of moisture-loving plants produce interest from early spring until autumn.

5 A richly organic soil is ideal for a bog garden. This is raked out evenly in a thick layer over the gravel.

6 The planting of pot-grown plants can take place at any time of the year. In the summer months they must be well watered until established. Allow sufficient space between the plants so that they can develop fully and for ease of maintenance.

PROJECT: A Wildlife Pool

Wildlife gardening aims to create places where animals and plants can thrive alongside humans in the domestic environment. A wildlife pool is normally constructed in the same way as a conventional garden pool, especially if the creation of a balanced eco-system is an objective. However, a layer of soil can be included on top of the liner so that plants can root directly into the soil rather than being confined in planting baskets.

The various depths of water necessary for the successful establishment of plants that will produce a balanced eco-system are essential. Marginal shelves should be provided to accommodate marginal aquatics, and deep water between 45 cm (18 in) and 90 cm (3 ft) depth is needed for waterlilies, other deep-water aquatics, and submerged plants, along with sufficient surface area for the free exchange of gases and the establishment of floating plants. Such conditions also provide all that is necessary for fish, snails, and amphibians.

A wildlife pool is not only about aquatic inhabitants and insect life; there are many birds which can be enjoyed at the pool side if provision is made for them. If a beach is constructed, then they can walk into the water and drink and bathe in the margins.

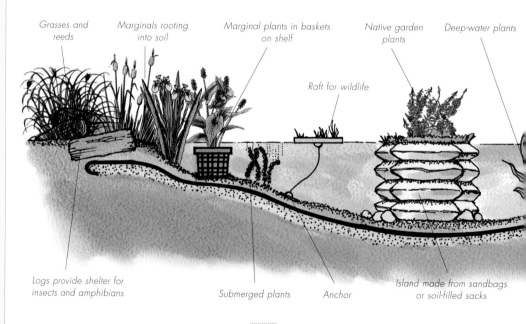

Grasses and reeds

Marginals rooting into soil

Marginal plants in baskets on shelf

Native garden plants

Deep-water plants

Raft for wildlife

Logs provide shelter for insects and amphibians

Submerged plants

Anchor

Island made from sandbags or soil-filled sacks

1 The addition of a beach extension to a lined pool is simple if done at the time of construction. Rake out soil from the excavation from intended water level to the bank.

2 Cut the underlay and spread it out from below the water level to the edge of the beach. Dampen it with water to assist with laying and cut off excess.

3 Mold the liner to the shape of the excavation, smoothing out as many creases as possible, and, if folds are needed, make them simple and generous.

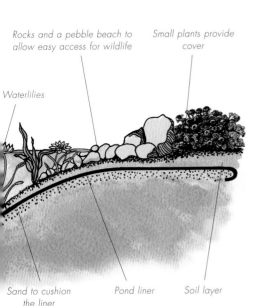

Rocks and a pebble beach to allow easy access for wildlife

Small plants provide cover

Waterlilies

Sand to cushion the liner

Pond liner

Soil layer

4 Tuck the liner under the turf, and, starting from the upper edge of the beach, use cobbles to create the surface. Use larger sizes at the top of the beach.

Above right: *The beach is complete. A beach gives birds an opportunity to drink and bathe. It also provides a simple exit for frogs and toads and an emergency exit for any adventurous hedgehogs.*

GETTING MORE AMBITIOUS

ADDING MOVING WATER

*M*oving water introduces a magical quality to a garden. Everyone, irrespective of age, is fascinated by water. The meandering stream, the purposeful rill and the tumbling waterfall all have their own special qualities. With the modern submersible pump it is relatively simple to bring such pleasures to the home garden.

However, a waterfall or cascade must be considered carefully. The whole mood of a garden is affected by the strength and flow of the moving water, together with the way that it catches the light. To create the best effect, the character of a waterfall or cascade in the garden should be copied from nature, even when it is not constructed from natural materials.

Whatever style is decided upon, be sure to integrate it properly into the garden landscape. There is always the danger of it appearing as an appendage to the water garden that has been imposed because of the gardener's desire for moving water. It must look as if it belongs.

A stream or rill is a tremendous asset to a garden. For the gardener who is fortunate enough to have a natural stream, there is likely to be little to do to improve its design or arrangement, although it may need altering slightly to be accommodated in the wider garden picture. The way in which a stream has contoured the landscape in its immediate vicinity may be appealing, but this has occurred over a long period of time without reference to what is around it.

When designing and constructing a stream from scratch, its potential for affecting other elements in the garden landscape should be taken into account before work commences.

Left: *No longer need moving water be confined to just a fountain or waterfall—nowadays, modernistic water-walls are becoming increasingly popular in the garden.*

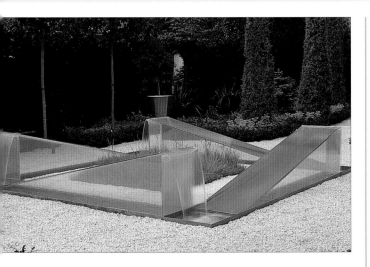

Tips & handy hints

When creating a waterfall, observe and learn from nature. The source of a natural waterfall is never from the highest point of a rock outcrop. A tall, slender fall of water draws the eye upwards, lengthening and narrowing the picture. A broad shallow fall widens it.

The sound and movement of water in a stream or rill can be adjusted by the variation of materials used for the stream-bed. A stream-bed covered with cobbles produces a different sound and effect than one covered with gravel or left bare.

Streams always look best when created in levels; in other words, when the stream-bed is level for a distance before dropping to another level. From time to time the pump will be switched off, so make sure that the various level sections retain a certain amount of water, thus not impairing the overall visual effect.

Top left: *This ingenious creation makes it appear as if the water is flowing uphill! Of course, it relies on an optical illusion.*

Left: *Remember that fast-moving water restricts the cultivation of quite a few aquatic plants.*

PROJECT: A Reservoir Pool

There is little difference in function between a header pool and a reservoir. The header pool is usually decorative and functional, while the reservoir is purely functional. Header pools are the small, shallow pools that serve to feed waterfalls. They are situated above a cascade or waterfall feature and water is directed into them via a hose from the pump. Although it is possible to grow some small aquatic plants in a header pool, it is not usually desirable either from the point of view of over-wintering or interference with maintenance.

Reservoirs are usually hidden from view. They mostly comprise tanks and are often completely enclosed. Solely functional, they offer opportunities for storing larger quantities of water than are available from a header pool. Reservoirs are not necessary at the summit of a waterfall or cascade, but they can provide a very useful service in the ground beneath a fountain or other moving water feature.

Sometimes a submersible pump is accommodated in a reservoir unit. This is particularly useful when the pool part of the water feature is of insufficient depth for the pump to function successfully or if the pump is going to be highly visible.

 If you plan to run a cable to a sump unit, make sure that it is buried safely under the surrounding soil.

1 Measure your reservoir and transfer the measurement to the ground by scoring the outline of the tank in the grass or soil.

4 Having excavated the hole to the required depth, now site the reservoir in it. Backfill around the edges with soil.

2 Cut around the mark created by the stick and line it with an edging iron or sharp spade to simplify turf lifting.

3 Remove the turf to slightly more than the exact circumference of the sump and dig down to the required depth.

5 Level the sump and then secure and support it with pea gravel backfilled between the sump walls and the ground.

6 Position the pump in the centre of the sump. You are now ready to fill the reservoir with water and cover it with its pre-formed lid.

PROJECT: A Pre-Formed Waterfall

There are many and varied pre-formed waterfall and cascade units that can be added to a pool. Some look very natural, but others are hideous, so take time to select appropriate units carefully and be aware of how much will still be exposed once they are installed.

Some pre-formed units are single structures, while others comprise a series of separate sections of different configuration which offer imaginative design opportunities. None of the pre-formed units, whether reconstituted stone, plastic or fibreglass, is easy to work with from the visual point of view. They really only look convincing when they are dressed with rocks and heavily planted. However, they are completely watertight.

Pre-formed waterfall and cascade units have to be installed on a slope. This may be a natural feature or else created by soil profiling, but should be both tall and wide enough to accommodate their length and breadth without looking cramped. If an artificial mound has to be created, it should ideally be allowed to settle over the winter period. Installing pre-formed units on freshly disturbed soil results in slippage, and the whole construction process may have to be started again. Pre-formed units can also be installed in a more formal manner where the land is terraced.

1 To avoid the outlet hose from the pump showing above the water, drill a small hole through the back, ideally below the point at which the water level will rest in the upper part of the unit.

2 It is vital to seal the joint with the input hose with a waterproof sealant so that there is no prospect of water escaping. Any seepage behind the unit may result in soil slippage.

3 Allow the sealant to set properly after introducing the fitting. The outlet pipe is trimmed so that the fitting can be fixed securely with a plastic nut screwed flush to the unit.

4 An excavation larger than the cascade units is prepared to permit room for adjustment. The units are then placed in their final positions.

5 The soil is then replaced carefully beneath and around the units. It is important that it fills all the voids and is packed down well.

6 When everything is in place and backfilled, it should be checked with a level. Also test the flow of water to see that it falls as you desire.

7 The finished feature planted with water flowing freely – a simple method of introducing moving water into the garden.

PROJECT: A Waterfall Using Liner

A pool liner offers the most flexible method of creating a waterfall or cascade. An excavation can be created and lined which reflects exactly the intentions of the designer.

The greatest danger with a liner construction is not so much the risk of puncturing, but seepage around the edges if these are not very carefully finished.

When excavating a liner waterfall, commence work next to the pool and then progress up the incline. As with a mound for pre-formed units, it is equally important that the soil into which the liner is to be placed is compacted. Any sinking after the liner is installed may result in seepage.

With a lined construction there are often facings of rock and a covering of gravel or shingle. These can be arranged to produce wonderful effects, but always remember that it is the solid soil foundation and the protective layer of pool liner that enable attractive natural-looking features to be created, and any deficiency will show later.

Dressing the finished construction with rocks and gravels also allows different flow patterns to be created. A curtain of water results from a smooth uniform edge while violent tumbles can be arranged by forcing the water through gaps in rocks and stones.

1 The soil is removed from a natural slope to create an excavation which is the finished size of the waterfall.

2 Line the excavation w underlay. This prevent stones or any other sharp objects from puncturing the liner.

3 Liner is spread o over the underla Ensure that there is sufficient over lap all round. Mould the liner to the trench.

4 Place the securing rocks firmly on the edge of the waterfall, creating as natural an appearance as possible.

5 Secure the lower rocks of the spillway with concrete. Set them firmly on a generous bed of mortar.

6 At vulnerable points along the spillway, point the rocks with mortar to prevent seepage. It is essential to cement the spillways at each part of the fall for an even flow.

7 When all the rocks are securely in place, any surplus pool liner should be cut off neatly. Edges can be disguised with topsoil. Well-washed gravel is introduced to the waterfall pools. This disguises wrinkles in the liner and creates a useful wildlife habitat.

Above: *A beautifully constructed waterfall using a liner and rocks. Spring bulbs and flowers have been planted to soften the contours of the rocky outline, and the result is a very pleasing natural-looking water feature.*

PROJECT: A Wooden Aqueduct

A canal or aqueduct is an exciting water garden feature, but one which really only fits into a formal garden design. It can be a feature for its own sake, or equally a means physically to separate parts of the garden. However it is contrived, it must have definite points to flow to and from. If creating a beginning and end point is not practical, then clever planting is necessary to ensure that it looks convincing.

A canal has to be very carefully blended into the garden design, especially with regard to the excavated soil. It may be simpler to dig out the canal and to place the soil on the banks, but this creates a very awkward and artificial appearance. A canal is often better partially excavated and then the soil spread up to the construction, or alternatively constructed at soil level with the water source and any pool level pre-determined, the ground being made up to the construction, rather than the canal sunk into the ground.

Canals can be constructed of a wide range of materials, but tile and wood are very serviceable and fashionable. Indeed, with the imaginative use of wood, narrow rills and spouts can easily be constructed that carry water in attractively symmetrical aqueducts. Brick is also satisfactory.

1 Prepare the timber carefully, ensuring a neat tight fit. Bond the timber edges to the base using a strong adhesive. Clamp the lengths in position until the adhesive has set. Accuracy of construction at this stage is very important.

2 Once the main timber components have been secured by a waterproof adhesive, they should be screwed together. Drill pilot holes slightly smaller than the screws and then screw them in

3 A small block of wood secures the end of the rill. This should be measured carefully and cut so that it can be glued and then screwed in

4 The whole unit can now be painted liberally with a wood preservative. Choose one that will prevent the timber from rotting and that will dry completely so that there is never any pollution hazard to the water.

5 A hole is drilled in the end stop board of the rill so that a small hose can be fed in to deliver the water. This outlet can be disguised with plants as the final picture (right) reveals.

Right: *Water from the rill tumbles into a reservoir trough where it is pumped back to the head of the aqueduct.*

PROJECT: A Small Stream and Cascade

Streams are best constructed from a pool liner that is disguised completely by rocks, pebbles, stones, and marginal planting. The first considerations with a stream are the header outlet and the base pool, for it is difficult to produce a credible independent stream without having a pool at the base in which a submersible pump can be placed and a small header feature to which the water can be pumped. The length of the stream and the ability of the pump to move the water the distance and vertical height required also needs careful thought because the efficiency of the pump drops off the greater the height of the head of water required and the length of hose through which the water is pumped.

The liner should ideally be all in one piece – rather than separate overlapping lengths – and it should be laid into a shallow excavation. It must also be spread well over the sides and tucked into the turf or concealed with edging material. Once lined, the stream bed should be heavily dressed with slabs of stone and pebbles. Similarly, large rocks and stones can be used to hide the sides of the stream, while occasionally, provision can be made for a marginal plant to be established to assist in the disguise of the stream edges.

Left: *An artificial stream is easier to manage than a real one – it can appear quite natural in the garden.*

 Mark out the outline of the streambed with stakes or string before digging commences. Dig the stream to the full depth, taking into account the required slope to the pond.

2 Line the excavated stream-bed with underlay, firming it down and ensuring that it moulds to the stream's contours. This will protect the liner when it is laid on top.

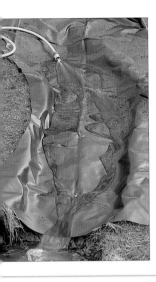

3 Lay the liner into the trench over the underlay and test that the water flow is satisfactory.

4 The pipe that carries the water to the head of the stream is laid in a thin trench.

5 Once the liner has been installed, the stones for the stream-bed are put in place.

6 The pool liner edge should be tucked under the turf to create a neat and tidy finish. Use large stones piled at the head of the stream to trap and conceal the outlet pipe.

7 Paddle stones are added to fill in any gaps between the larger slabs on the stream-bed. Lower the pump into the pool close to the stream. It will need to be quite powerful.

FUN WITH FOUNTAINS

*F*or generations, fountains have decorated the ponds of the world's great gardens, but it is only in recent times that they have become available in an economical and readily available form for the home gardener. With the advent of the modern submersible pump, fountains have been brought within the reach of us all. Its compactness, power, and versatility have made possible water acrobatics that in the past would have been both difficult and expensive to create.

Above: *The innovative gardener can produce a fountain feature using eye-catching, unconventional materials.*

Left: *The traditional fountain ornament feature is still a favorite. The use of resin-bonded materials has made them relatively inexpensive to purchase.*

The position in which a fountain is placed should be carefully chosen. It is important to take into account the spread of the spray in relation to the pond as well as the effects of light and shade. A fountain should be placed in a sunny spot with the main viewing point in the shade in order to accentuate the feature. It is also important to consider how the fountain jet will appear against various backgrounds, these usually varying considerably according to viewing point.

There are many opportunities for creating an impact, for there is an enormous selection of spray patterns from which to choose.

Tips & handy hints

With a multi-jet fountain there is the added potential to enjoy the effects of light passing through water and providing glistening sprays. By placing the fountain where it will receive the maximum direct sunlight, it is possible to enjoy the magical qualities of light meeting the water for most of the day and from various viewpoints.

A fountain should be regarded as an embellishment to the design of a water feature, providing flowing contours, sound, movement and light. A tall fountain jet will lift the eye, a broad multi-jet will attract light and concentrates the eye at a lower level.

The greatest enemy of a fountain is the wind. A draughty position should be avoided. Choose a sunny site which is sheltered from the prevailing wind.

Above: *The regularity of the spray patterns here serves to emphasize the formal symmetry of this feature.*

There is no need to decide upon a single one, for the jets are readily interchangeable, being merely pushed on top of the pump outlet. However, remember that a fountain that emanates directly from the water's surface will only be a feature while the pump is switched on. One produced from an ornament remains a focal point. A fountain without an ornament produces a totally different picture, because the pond suddenly becomes flat and mirror-like when it is off.

PROJECT: A Pond Fountain On A Plinth

The installation of a fountain in a pond is relatively simple if a modern submersible pump is utilized. Considerable output can be achieved by a small pump which is discrete and easy to hide. Sometimes a pump may be situated conveniently immediately beneath a fountain ornament, rocks or other decorative features. This is generally the most satisfactory arrangement, as the water is then delivered for the shortest distance.

It is possible to install a pump which takes water to a remote spray head, but full account must be taken of the distance the water has to travel and the strength of pump necessary both to move the water and to produce the desired spray effect. In such circumstances it is necessary to disguise the pump.

It is essential that the pump is both level and accessible. It should be possible regularly to remove and clean the input filter, as debris getting into the water flow and blocking the fountain jet is one of the greatest irritations for the pond owner. The electrical cable must also be dealt with safely and carefully, wherever possible its exit point from the pool being situated beneath a carefully placed rock or paver at the water's edge.

Different heads produce different spray patterns, allowing you a quick way to change the look of the pool.

1 When preparing a plinth for a fountain, it is important to work out the scale of the construction and to calculate the height at which the pump must be situated to create the desired effect. To protect the pool liner, cushioning liner underlay should be laid before construction of the plinth begins.

4 The pump should be level on the plinth. The plinth can also support a fountain ornament with the pump hidden beneath.

2 A paving slab having being laid and levelled as the foundation, work can begin. Ordinary house bricks are laid using a standard mortar. For a plinth up to three bricks high, you may lay the bricks directly upon one another. Larger ones require staggered brickwork.

3 The top of the plinth is made from a paving slab. It is very important that this is absolutely level from side to side and end to end in order that the pump sits evenly and securely.

5 You can use a hook secured to a stick to lower the pump onto the plinth if you do not want to wade into the water to do this.

6 With the pump installed, it is simply a matter of plugging it into the electricity supply and switching on. Providing that the jet is positioned just clear of the water surface, the fountain will swing into full and effective action immediately.

PROJECT: A Wall Fountain

Wall fountains provide a very versatile method of introducing moving water into the smaller garden without diminishing its importance. Apart from masks and gargoyles, there are many types of wall fountains which are completely self-contained and flow into a raised or sunken basal pool, a bowl or dish.

Wall masks and gargoyles are available in all sorts of styles and in materials ranging from reconstituted stone and lead to terracotta, fiberglass, and plastic. Their appearance is obviously important, but so is that of the container into which the water is to spout. This must be of a size and capacity which will accommodate the spray, but also be of a pleasing appearance and in visual conformity with its surroundings.

Consideration must also be given to the wall to which the fountain is attached. Old solid walls create difficulty with disguising the discharge pipe from the pump, and chasing a groove into the wall is often the only option. Unless carefully undertaken, this can look ugly. The ideal is to attach the fountain to a cavity wall and take the pipe up through the cavity where it will be out of sight. When all else fails, use an attractive pipe as a virtue.

Above: *An attractive arrangement for a small garden with plenty of opportunities for enjoying plants, fish and the magic of moving water*

1 Masks and gargoyles are not the easiest features to fit successfully. Plan to make all the connections in mock-up first before drilling the holes in the wall and committing to its fixing. Make sure that all the connections and the screw holes function before fitting begins.

2 Mark the positions precisely, holding the mask in position against the wall. Once the drilling points have been established, drill the holes and insert suitable plugs. They expand as the screws are inserted and hold the mask to the wall.

3 Secure the mask firmly in place, making certain that all the pipe work and connections on the other side of the wall are in the correct position.

4 There are usually covers or caps provided to disguise the screw heads and to conceal the method of fastening. Fit these and make sure that they are secure, sealing as necessary.

5 Connect the pump to the outlet and place it in position in the reservoir pool, disguising the outflow pipe at the same time. It is prudent to check water output at this time. Add suitable plants. Take account of the water level and only introduce those that are compatible and equal in size. Select only those plants that do not object to constantly splashing water.

PROJECT: A Poolside Cascade

Moving water usually emanates from within the pond or else tumbles over a

waterfall or cascade, but it is also perfectly possible to arrange for it to feature at the side of the pond. The submersible pump is placed within the pond and the delivery hose carried to the top of the feature in much the same way as with a waterfall. Poolside features are often formal and take the form of a raised tube or chute, or ornamental fountain heads. In such cases considerable quantities of water are moved and the splash resulting from such water displacement is considerable. This should be considered very carefully from the beginning. Less formal arrangements – particularly units or features that are manufactured for the purpose and where a gentle flow of water is preferred – are much easier to install.

At present there is a trend for creating leaves in fibreglass with connections and jets which enable them to be arranged rather like an artificial plant with water tumbling from leaf to leaf. On their own, even if arranged in natural array, they look rather stiff and fake, but once fully integrated with live vegetation they can be very pleasing, creating subtle sounds and movement of water.

1 Drill a hole in the leaf to accommodate the outflow pipe in the base of the Gunnera. Use a holesaw drill fitting.

2 Insert a screw fitting and secure the outflow pipe from beneath with a clip. To ensure that it attaches firmly, use a quick-setting bonding agent. It is important that the union between leaf and pipe is secure. Any seepage will reduce the flow rate.

3 Secure the outflow pipe to the pump outlet using a jubilee clip. Ensure that only the waterfall outflow is functional and make an adjustments necessary to the control valve to eliminate flow to the fountain.

4 It is possible to enhance the appearance
of the leaf by using a spray paint aerosol.
Use sparingly to create a subtle effect.

5 Having placed the first leaf, it is essential
to test the water flow using a watering
can to ensure that it pours out as desired.

6 The second
leaf is placed
in position.
Then put the
pump in the
pond, conceal
the pipework
with plants,
and switch on.

Above: *Even artificial leaves can look effective. They are a very
practical way of bringing tumbling water into the garden.*

Decking and Bridges

Wooden decking can be used very successfully to hide the pond edge or to produce a viewing or landing platform. It is usual for decking to extend over the pondside, but it need not project too much. This ensures that it can be secured successfully to the surrounding ground rather than any construction having to take place within the pond itself. Irrespective of the construction method used, decking is most effective if positioned just above the surface of the water.

With most water features, decking runs along the edge of the pond in a fairly narrow strip, rather like a causeway. It is very versatile and especially useful with formal water features, although there are occasions when it works well in informal surroundings too. Hardwood is the most satisfactory construction material, not only being very weather-resistant, but also mellowing to a pleasant silver-grey color with age.

Bridges not only provide a means of crossing water, but also allow the water

Below: *The encircling of this pond with decking provides a neat finish to the edge and a generous area for sitting out and enjoying the fish and other pond life.*

Tips & handy hints

Crossing water by a bridge or causeway allows the water garden to be seen from another viewpoint. Make the most of this by arranging the planting to provide focal points that are not visible from the edge.

The arrangement of boards on a causeway affects the visitor's behaviour. When they are placed lengthways there is an encouragement to cross; when arranged widthways there is the temptation to linger.

If a bridge is going to be principally a focal point, rather than simply functional, design the stream to meander beneath it. Choose the best site for the bridge and then create the course of the stream.

Above: *A simple wooden causeway enables the pond to be enjoyed from a completely different viewpoint.*

Below: *Apart from physically crossing water, a carefully designed bridge can also become a valuable focal point.*

garden to be viewed from a different perspective. Sometimes, as is common with Japanese style gardens, the bridge is constructed principally as a focal point.

A causeway is an alternative to a bridge, although it may not always take the visitor by the most direct route. The main attraction of the causeway is the range of experiences that it can offer as it wends its way across the water. Amongst these is the opportunity for the visitor to walk comfortably and dry-shod among reeds and rushes growing in the pond.

PROJECT: Making Decking

When it comes to making your own decking, the first and most important consideration is to purchase the best quality timber that you can afford. Cheap timber that is only sparingly treated with preservative not only looks poor, but it will have a very limited life.

It is vital to ensure that all supports for decking are substantial; timber uprights should be at least 10 cm (4 in) square and either set in concrete or dropped into a metal fencing sleeve or pipes set into concrete. The maximum distance between structural posts should be 180 cm (6 ft).

The boards themselves are mostly 15 cm (6 in) wide, although it is possible to get both narrower and wider deckboards. The gap between boards when they are fastened to the subframe should be no more than 5 mm (0.2 in); make sure that whatever gap you leave is consistent across the whole deck. The space permits the timber to move in different weather conditions and lets rainwater drain away freely.

Decking screws are now widely available and are the best method of securing the timbers to their supports, although there is still a place for bolts, especially where strong uprights require connecting. Alternatively galvanized deck ties can be used to secure boards to the joists.

Always use quality timber for a job that will last.

1 The timber framework for decking should be substantial and the individual bearers placed at intervals to provide good support. These should be set no more than 45 cm (18 in) apart, but ideally 30 cm (12 in), especially over water.

2 Having ensured that the framework is square and tightly secured, the first deckboard is placed in position at the desired angle. Start at one corner of the framework and work outwards.

3 Secure the first board using decking
screws. These are best screwed in using
a power screwdriver. Prior to fastening it
down, square off each end of this board
so that it will lie flush with the frame.

4 Position the boards so that a straight
edge can be placed on them and
the angle at which each has to be cut can
be marked with a pencil line. Ensure a small
gap between each for subsequent fixing.

5 The gap between
boards to allow for
timber movement and
surface drainage need
only be minimal, but it
should be uniform.
The end of a
carpenter's pencil can
be utilized as a
convenient unit of
measurement.

6 The boards are placed in position and secured
with decking screws, at least two being used at
each support point. It is important to ensure that
they screw vertically into the timber for a secure fit.

7 There is usually a small carpentry task required at
the end to ensure a neat finish. It is possible to
run the decking out to an even number of boards,
but this rarely produces ideal overall dimensions.

PROJECT: Using Ready-Made Decking

In the past, decking was often overwhelmingly linear in appearance and construction. All the boards ran in the same direction. However, with the increasing and widespread use of decking, especially in Europe and the USA, manufacturers and designers have appreciated that decking need not be simply functional, but can be an integral part of the designed landscape, making a major visual contribution to the outside living space.

The problem remained, however, that if limited to using just straight lengths of timber, the home gardener would have to be a skilled carpenter to achieve interesting patterns and variations that would have a powerful visual impact. Realizing the limitations of the average home handyman, manufacturers have now come up with ready-made decking shapes in a series of appealing patterns and configurations. Squares of decking are the most popular, but hexagons, octagons, circles, and other shapes are now freely available, many of which can be mixed and matched with one another. Elaborate features can be easily realized with modern decking squares.

While these can be used as part of traditional decking construction, they are also versatile enough to be attractively arranged to create landing stages and piers, the fixing arrangements being identical to those used for conventional decking construction, but with additional supports when several shapes are utilized together.

1 Measure and cut the support timbers so that they correspond exactly with the dimensions of the decking square.

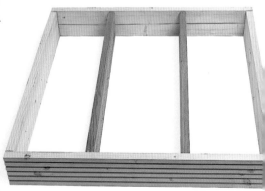

2 Once cut to length, position the timbers in a square and check that the decking top fits exactly. Then screw the base together.

3 Provide central bearers to ensure that the platform is fully supported. Once the legs are secured, these will be screwed into position.

4 Using decking screws, fasten the boards that form the edge of the platform to the support legs. The framework can now be fastened together before the ready-made decking section is fitted on top of it.

5 The ready-made decking square is now ready for securing to the platform framework.

6 Fasten the decking square using decking screws. It will fit snugly on the top of the support.

Below: When installed, ensure that the platform is level.

PROJECT: A Wooden Causeway

A wooden bridge or causeway provides an opportunity to see the water garden from another angle. Although they should be visually appealing, most wooden bridges are first and foremost functional. They are used rather than viewed.

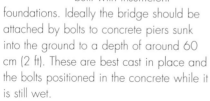

Any bridge or causeway construction must have a secure foundation. This is not only necessary for the safe passage of people, but also ensures stability. Even a modest bridge can settle under its own weight if it is built with insufficient foundations. Ideally the bridge should be attached by bolts to concrete piers sunk into the ground to a depth of around 60 cm (2 ft). These are best cast in place and the bolts positioned in the concrete while it is still wet.

The simplest method of creating supports for a causeway is to set short lengths of pipe into a concrete slab, or to bolt metal post supports to sturdy breeze blocks. The wooden supports for the bearers that will carry the planks of the causeway are dropped into these pipes after positioning in the pond. When such piers are created in a lined pool, it is important that they rest on a generous layer of fleece underlay to prevent damage to the liner.

1 It is essential to have bolts firmly secured into the concrete basal supports.

2 Bolt the metal sleeves that will hold the bridge supports securely to the base.

3 Put the timber supports into the metal sleeves and make sure they are vertical. Clamp a cross-member to each upright, making sure that it is level. Use this as a template for the positioning of the other supports.

4 Secure each cross-piece with bolts in pre-drilled counter-sunk holes. All cross-members and supports must align.

5 Drill the lengths of timber that are to form the walk-way and secure them to the supports using substantial bolts.

6 Where there is a change in alignment of the causeway, make provision for the boards to fit neatly and evenly together.

Right: *The completed causeway – a neat and very economical method of bridging water attractively.*

PROJECT: An Arched Bridge

It is quite feasible to build an arched bridge from scratch, but it is more usual to purchase such a feature either ready-made or as a kit for self-assembly. Even modest bridges are a considerable weight and must have sound foundations from both the point of view of safety and gradual settlement. If the soil slips, the bridge can twist and be damaged. So it is imperative that the positions of both ends of the bridge are thoroughly inspected and that suitable piers can be constructed to take the weight securely.

To be safe, the footings for each pier should be excavated to a depth of 60 cm (2 ft). Bridge piers can be pre-cast, but it can be simpler in most cases to cast them in position. For most bridges, digging holes of sufficient dimensions and filling them with concrete is adequate. Take care on clay soils which shrink badly, and, where appropriate, include reinforcing rods in the piers.

When pre-cast piers are used, dig the holes at least 15 cm (6 in) larger allround than the piers themselves. Place them in position and pour in concrete. Alternatively, you can build brick piers in the manner illustrated. Check that the piers on either bank are level and then install the bridge.

1 Create a level base for pier construction using mortar. Lay bricks in an alternate arrangement to create piers.

2 Decide where the uprights will fit and mark the section of board that will have to be removed. Cut out the slots that will accommodate the uprights for the curved handrail.

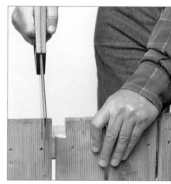

3 Screw the components together using rust-proof decking screws The uprights should be evenly spaced along the bridge.

4 Fasten the handrail securely. Ensure that the screws are countersunk for safety.

5 Drill holes through the base of the bridge to accommodate long screws. Change to a masonry drill bit when the drill reaches the bricks.

6 Insert long masonry fixings into the holes. Then, screw the bridge securely to the brick piers.

Above: *There are a variety of wood paints for garden features that can be used to decorate small bridges like this.*

PROJECT: Stepping Stones

Stepping stones are almost inevitably placed after construction has been completed and water added to the feature. In the case of a natural watercourse, it is difficult to assess their ideal position accurately with regard to depth unless water is flowing freely and at an average depth. However, this can create difficulties with installation, as stepping stones are ideally placed when the water is at its lowest level. The perfect solution with a naturally variable water course is to take average water depth measurements and then position the stepping stones at a time of minimal flow.

In an artificial situation this is not a problem. Water levels are either known, or if uncertain are tested, and then the stepping stones installed appropriately. The relationship of the surface of the stones to the level of the water can be easily assessed.

Whether the installation of stepping stones is to take place in an artificial stream or pond, or in order to traverse a natural flow of water, stability is essential. The stones must be securely concreted or affixed to a level base and positioned sufficiently close to one another so that anyone crossing can do so with a normal gait. Take care to choose stones that have a naturally roughened surface – smooth surfaces are likely to become slippery when wet.

A stepping stone is rather like an iceberg, the majority of the structure being beneath the water. A strong construction of this kind is absolutely essential to ensure personal safety.

1 A generous mortar bed must be laid to enable a level brick base for each stepping stone to be constructed.

2 Start by positioning bricks in the corners. Ensure that these are set square. This base should be smaller than the stepping stone.

3 Continue construction with the joints of the bricks arranged in an alternate fashion. Check regularly to ensure that they are level.

4 A final layer of mortar is applied when the desired height has been reached in order to secure the stepping stone.

5 Place the stepping stone gently into position on the mortar bed and firm it into place. There should be a slight overhang.

6 Tap the stepping stone gently into position and make sure that it is level. Remove any surplus mortar.

ISLANDS AND LIGHTS

Islands are not suitable for all water gardens, although with larger water features they are, for the most part, welcome additions. Wildlife ponds in particular benefit from an island, even if of quite modest proportions. This provides a safe refuge from predators for vulnerable wildlife, especially nesting birds.

On some occasions it is desirable to create the island at the same time as the water feature. However, for most gardeners, constructing the island in a finished pond is the most satisfactory option. An island can be a wet island for colonizing by moisture-loving plants, or a dry island for conventional decorative garden subjects – it depends upon the method of construction.

Floating islands are another possibility, and are particularly useful with a wildlife feature. Constructed on a wooden pallet and planted appropriately, they are especially popular with nesting waterfowl. They are anchored to the floor of the pond and provide the additional benefit of surface shade for fish and other aquatic life, which also enjoy exploring the trailing plant roots hanging in the water beneath.

Garden lighting can greatly enhance a water feature. There are several different kinds of light available, each for a specific purpose. Underwater lighting is useful for illuminating moving features like fountains and waterfalls, while single and multiple spotlights, often with interchangeable coloured lenses, are perfect for highlighting, silhouetting and shadowing garden features around the pond. There are also lighting systems for moonlighting, creating a particularly lovely effect upon the uncluttered glassy stillness of the surface of a pond.

Left: *The underwater spotlight highlights and dramatizes the point at which the falling curtain of water enters the pond.*

Tips & handy hints

With a wet island, always use soil that is not rich in nutrients, as these are likely to leach back into the pool and encourage the appearance of a green algal bloom. A wet island need not be made entirely of soil; the lower half can be filled with brick rubble.

Illuminate a waterfall from the entry point of the cascade of water. The lamp is then shielded by the luminescence, while the beam is directed up into the flow. Front lighting a waterfall often results in the light beam bouncing back.

When lighting a fountain ornament, place the light slightly to the side, illuminating it in profile. Front-on lighting gives a flat and displeasing appearance. Where shadows create a problem, always direct the light beam at the point at which the water emerges.

Left: *An island need not always be large, nor a home for moisture-loving or aquatic plants. Dry islands can accommodate traditional garden plants, a small tree here providing an interesting feature in a modern pond.*

PROJECT: In-pool Lighting

It is vital when installing lighting to have a very healthy respect for electricity, especially when it is in close proximity to water. Potentially this is a deadly combination. However, there should be no problem with in-pond lights providing that a reputable brand is purchased and all the instructions that are given with the equipment are adhered to properly.

Underwater lighting is quite safe – modern units are manufactured to operate with low-voltage cable and a transformer, and the light units themselves are specially sealed. For the best effect, underwater lighting can be placed beneath a fountain or waterfall feature to illuminate the tumbling water. Alternatively it can be situated at the edge of the pool, pointing inwards to focus upon a particular ornament or plant grouping, or outwards to illuminate an object on the pond edge. The placement of lights is not an exact science, and it may be necessary to reposition the lights several times before the desired effect is achieved.

Some fountains have integral lights, which do not require any particular installation skills. However, it is important to position the fountain feature and pump on a secure flat plinth, and ideally in a position where the cable can be discreetly hidden as it enters the pond.

Above: *In-pool lighting can be most effective when used to highlight specific plants or pond ornaments. It is safe to use and available in a wide range of packages. Most have a transformer and a choice of clip-on colored lenses* **(below)**.

94

1 One of the most effective lighting arrangements simply clips the spotlight to a pump beneath the fountain head.

2 The color of the light can be changed by the use of differently colored lenses which snap on to make a watertight seal.

3 The submersible pump and lights are placed into position in the pool. The lights point upwards beneath the fountain.

4 When switched on, the light should illuminate all the spray pattern. Slight adjustment of the lights may be necessary.

PROJECT: External Lighting

Most exterior garden lights are installed after construction of the water feature is complete. Indeed, it is often not until the pond is up and working that lighting is considered. It can then be tricky to achieve exactly the desired effect. It is better to regard lighting as an integral part of the project from the outset so that any mains cabling or weatherproof power sockets can be carefully incorporated into the original plan.

Water and electricity are not compatible in most situations, so it is important to use only purpose-designed outdoor lighting and to follow installation instructions to the letter. Most outdoor garden lighting systems operate from a transformer that is linked to the normal domestic electrical supply. The transformer reduces the voltage to a safe level, which means that the low-voltage cables from the transformer to the light units can be run quite safely along the surface of the ground, or concealed amongst the surrounding plants.

Once the positioning of the lights has been determined, it may be considered desirable to bury the cable so that it does not catch on a hoe or fork while you are undertaking routine tasks in the garden. In this case, use conduit to thread it through and install in a similar way to the method illustrated which is recommended for armored cables.

1 The modern garden lighting kit is safe and reliable. However, follow instructions at all times – don't be tempted to improvise.

2 A transformer ensures that the electrical power output into the garden is stepped down to a safe voltage.

3 When fixing the lights, determine the position you want them to be and then screw the connectors into the cable.

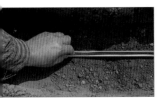  

4 Any external cable carrying mains power should be of a waterproof armored kind and laid in a conduit in a trench.

5 Plastic cable conduits have snap-on covers that keep the wire safe from any disturbance by spade or fork.

6 Once the conduit is securely positioned in the foot of the trench, cover it over with a generous layer of sand.

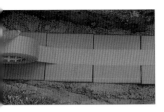

7 Cover the cable with tiles for additional protection. Stretch electrical hazard tape along the run of tiles. This gives immediate warning of danger in case it should be unearthed.

8 The individual lights are set up at the poolside and focused upon carefully selected features in the pond.

Above: *An entire water feature can be lit to give a dramatic appearance at night. Alternatively, waterfalls, fountains or bridges can be selectively highlighted.*

PROJECT: A Dry Island

The simplest island to construct for the formal pool is one made of brick. One of the main advantages of a brick island over any other form of

construction is that it can be built as a dry island. That is one where the planting area within is drier than the marginal shelves or bog garden around the pond.

The bricks are laid in a conventional fashion to create a box-like effect, the lower layer being laid on fleece underlay positioned on top of the liner. When the island's position is known well in advance, a solid slab or foundation can be positioned beneath the pond liner as the feature is being built to provide a secure base.

A brick island has to be relatively tall to stand above the water, and this quite naturally leaves a cavernous space within. However, it does not have to be totally filled with soil or compost, although many gardeners prefer to do so. The bottom half or third can consist of hardcore. If you want to make sure that the island is impermeable to seepage through the bricks, a membrane can then be placed on top of this and subsequently brought up the sides as an inner liner.

1 When a brick structure is built in a lined pool, it is a wise precaution to install a support slab beneath the liner.

2 Lay a generous bed of mortar for the first layer of bricks and ensure that they are both square and level.

3 The ends of the bricks must be 'buttered' with mortar to fill the gaps between them. Lay the bricks in an alternate arrangement and ensure that each layer is level, square and vertical.

4 Once the mortar has dried thoroughly, a waterproofing sealant can be applied to the inner surfaces.

5 Fill the lower third of the structure with hardcore or gravel to provide drainage. Then fill the remainder with soil.

6 Choose suitable garden plants of varying flowering periods and plant as in the open garden. Here a shrub provides the focus.

7 A heavily planted dry island such as this benefits from regular annual lifting and replanting to keep it looking fresh.

PROJECT: A Wet Island

One of the easiest and most effective islands to create is one built of sandbags. Sandbags are readily available from builders' merchants and can be filled with either sand or soil as desired. Sand is more easily shaped and, although it is significantly heavier than soil, it does not contain nutrients which might escape into the water and create an algae problem. On the other hand, the island is never going to become a real one from the plants' point of view, for roots are not going to penetrate the sand significantly and bind the island together. Indeed, a few years down the road, if not properly maintained with a consistent level of water, the hessian may rot, the sand spill out and the island disintegrate.

Soil in the bags will be bound together by roots and become a solid island, but there are considerable hazards of the nutrients in the soil leaching out into the surrounding water. The plants which will be established on sandbag islands will be bog or marginal subjects. A sandbag island is a wet island, the water table being at the level of the water in the pond which surrounds it, and so marginal and bog plants will thrive in this damp habitat.

Planted island features require replanting every second year if they are to retain their character.

1 Fill sandbags with river sand. Ensure that they are all of consistent size and shape.

2 Arrange the sandbags rather like bricks in alternate fashion to form a solid construction.

3 Complete the structure so that the sandbags at the top are just at final water level.

4 Fill the lower part of the island, where the plant roots are unlikely to penetrate, with hardcore.

5 Top up the central part of the island with suitable compost. Aquatic planting compost is the best medium to use.

6 Plant towards the edge of the island using trailing plants that will hang over the side and disguise the sandbags. Space these equally around the edge.

7 Fill the center of the planting area with taller plants. Avoid invasive species which will crowd the center.

PROJECT: A Planted Raft

There are a number of ways of constructing an island, but a floating feature is amongst the most attractive and versatile. Rather like a boat,

it can be hauled to shore for regular maintenance. As a result of the way in which the plants are inserted into the growing medium, it is quite easy to make planting adjustments and changes when necessary.

The main part of the structure is a wooden pallet. If a full-size pallet is too large, then it is possible to reduce the size by sawing off a section. Provided that support rails are present at each side and ideally through the middle, then the pallet will remain secure and balanced.

The simplest buoyancy aids are empty plastic drinks bottles. Provided that the tops are securely screwed on, they are most effective. The bottles are inserted into the gaps between the slats on the pallet in an even arrangement, ensuring that there is sufficient space to accommodate the growing medium. The whole bottom of the pallet can be covered with pond liner to make a container into which compost can be spooned, and the top of the raft clad in burlap. Young plants and rooted cuttings are then planted through slits made in the material.

1 Use a wooden pallet and, if necessary, shorten it to the desired size. Use empty soft drinks bottles pushed between the timbers to provide buoyancy.

4 Provide added support beneath to take the weight of compost by adding further strengthening timbers. Then add an equal mixture (by volume) of aquatic compost and multipurpose potting compost.

2 Cover the base of the pallet with pool liner, pull this taut, and then cover it with chicken wire. This creates a watertight compartment which will accommodate the growing medium.

3 Secure the liner at the sides with timber. This holds all the bottles for buoyancy firmly in position.

5 Cover the surface of the pallet tightly with burlap or sacking. Secure this at the edges of the pallet with large-headed felt nails. Cut holes in the burlap that are large enough to accommodate the small rootballs of young aquatic plants.

6 Push bare-rooted plants into the compost through the holes in the burlap and water thoroughly. Cut back any that are unstable. Complete the planting arrangement using a combination of marginal and flowering and foliage bog garden plants.

EDGING THE POOL

*H*ow the edge of a pond or water feature is treated largely determines its visual success. The point where water meets dry ground is critical, not only structurally, but visually, for it demands either a strong statement or a soft disguise. It is also at this point that the structure of the water feature is at its most vulnerable, the point at which the liner or construction material joins the rest of the garden landscape.

In a formal situation the treatment must be decisive. Either a straight line, a mathematical curve or circle to define or accentuate the pond outline are desirable. Hard landscaping materials such as paving and bricks are often used, frequently in a formal and decorative association with cobbles or pebbles.

With an informal water feature, the planted edge is always to be preferred visually, with perhaps a single access point

Right: *Brick pavers provide a very neat traditional edge that suits a formal water feature well.*

Below: *This imaginative pool features a pleasing variety of edging – paddle stones extend down into the water, while planted borders soften the perimeter lines.*

Tips & handy hints

It is important when paving the edge of a pond to allow for at least 5 cm (2 in) of overhang. This enables a neat, even edge to be created and helps to obscure the top of the pond wall from view. With a lined pool it also helps to protect the liner wall between the surface and the edge from excessive and possibly damaging exposure to UV rays.

Whatever type of pond edging material is decided upon, remember that safety must come first. Visitors to the poolside must be guaranteed a sure and solid footing.

Grass makes a pleasing edge to a pool, but can become very untidy and difficult to manage at the waterside. It helps to use a base of rockwool for the grass to grow on to make a clean edge (see pages 112-113).

o view the pond and feed the fish. The plants should not be so tall that they spoil the overall aspect of the pond, nor so garish that they detract from the focus of clear water and colorful floating waterlilies.

In most cases good soil binding and scrambling plants, which disguise the union of pond and garden, are ideal, either extending down into the water from their home on dry land or tumbling out of the marginal shelves. With a wildlife pond such plants can sometimes be a little over-exuberant, and so a cobble beach may be considered as an alternative.

PROJECT: Edging With Stone

Edging with stones, slabs and bricks looks most effective around a formal pond. It is sensible to work out the requirements for all the elements from the beginning. There is nothing more irritating than to construct a pond, only to find when the paving comes to be laid that one slab has to be cut on each side in order to finish the edging evenly.

Levels are also important. The pool should be level from side to side and end to end, the surrounding land having also been levelled to accommodate the paving. When laid, the slabs or bricks should also be level from side to side and end to end if the finished result is to be both functional and satisfying visually. Remember to leave sufficient width of liner around the margins of the pool so that the paving stones can anchor the liner securely.

Safety is very important. A loose slab can tip an unwary visitor into the pond, so sufficient mortar of suitable strength must be used to ensure that the slabs are bedded down securely and do not move when trodden on.

1 Lay a generous, even bed of mortar close to the edge of the pool for securing the paving.

2 Lay the paving stones on the mortar bed with a slight overhang. This neatens the edge.

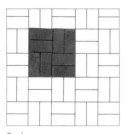

Basket weave

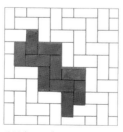

90° herringbone

45° herringbone

In a formal situation, it can be satisfying to edge a pond with bricks laid in a variety of symmetrical patterns. The 45° herringbone pattern is very striking, but hard to work with at the pool's edge.

3 The second row of paving stones can be used to secure the edge of the liner in position.

4 Cut off any surplus liner and firm the second row of paving securely on the mortar bed.

5 Brush a dry mortar mix into the joints between the paving stones, taking care not to let any drop into the pond. Water gently to ensure that it will set properly.

6 When the edge is complete, wash off any mortar splashes. Tie the water feature to the garden landscape by using cobbles or laying turf up to the paving stone edging.

PROJECT: Edging With A Beach

With the popularity of wildlife ponds, the cobble beach has come into its own. It is not only seen as a method of edging the pond attractively, but also as providing a ready access for wildlife, especially birds, to enjoy the watery world. It also serves as an exit for small animals which might fall into the pond, but which can then clamber to safety.

An effective method of constructing a beach is firstly to excavate a shallow, sloping incline at one of the margins of the pond. The liner should be stretched over this area and then secured. If the beach is not just for birds and is going to take some pressure from foot traffic, then a shallow concrete footing can be made to trap the liner. This should be continuous for the length of the beach and immovable.

Where bricks are being used, the liner should be pulled tight and secured. The area in front and behind the bricks or footing can then be covered with cobbles to create an informal look, and this arrangement of stones then extended to the water's edge.

Wildlife will especially appreciate a cobble beach next to a pond. It allows easy access to the water.

1 Secure the liner with turf or an edge of bricks. This is essential and provides a solid base upon which the beach is constructed.

2 It is advisable to lay at least two rows of bricks. The liner can then be trapped in place between them.

3 Once the mortar has set, cobbles can be added the larger ones being positioned first and covering the bricks.

4 A mixture of well-washed pebbles and cobbles can then be added and heaped up to depth of 15 to 20 cm (6-8 in).

5 To prevent cobbles from rolling into the bottom of the pool, create a barrier using larger stones. These will be totally submerged.

Below: A cobble beach provides a natural, visually appealing, and easily maintained transition from lawn to pond.

PROJECT: Timber Edging

Timber is not as permanent a solution to edging a pond as paving, but it does have its uses. When a pond is being constructed in conjunction with timber decking, then timber edging is a natural extension of the feature. It is also a good way of completing raised pools of timber construction, such as those made from railway

sleepers and liner. It also looks appropriate in rustic settings, even though the wood is prepared and treated formally.

There are a number of ways of fixing timber, these depending upon the visual effect that it is desired. When the surface of the soil is to be level with the surrounding ground, then an innovative system must be employed with a specially constructed concrete surround being built into which the timber can be bolted. The liner is trapped between this timber and wooden edging that will rest just in the water. Timber plating joints are used to hold the two wooden sections tightly together. Their screws do not penetrate the liner and allow the water to come right to the top without seepage. Providing that the timber edging is treated with preservative, it will make a durable and fine-looking edging.

Apart from the horizontal use of timber edging, the upright log-roll type of material so frequently used for edging and creating flower beds can also be pressed into use using similar methods of fixing. It is useful in informal surroundings, as it can follow the curves and bends of a pool.

1 A raised wooden pond can be successfully edged with timber, but protective underlay is advisable to prevent the liner from rubbing.

USING TIMBER

The use of timber as an edging is ideal for the do-it-yourself enthusiast. Modern timbers for garden use are now widely available already treated with a preservative. It is important for a high quality finish to use good tools and to measure accurately.

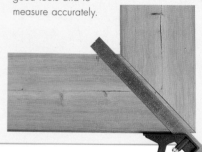

2 Pull the liner tightly over the pool edge, smoothing out the wrinkles and creating bold folds of liner to take up the slack.

3 Screw the timber edging securely to the pool framework. It is advisable to use decking screws, as these are rustproof.

4 Cut off the surplus liner. Allow for a small overhang so that the final trimming of the

5 There are many attractive wood stains and preservatives available which are quite safe to use in close proximity to water.

PROJECT: Turf and Rockwool Edging

Grass can be a most effective natural edging and, although it does present a few minor maintenance problems, it is well worth considering in a natural setting. The important consideration with a traditional turf edging is the depth of soil required up to the edge of the pond to maintain the health of the grass. To ensure that grass edging does not dry out, it is necessary to have a minimum depth of 5 cm (2 in) of soil, although 10 cm (4 in) is preferable.

If the grass is laid as turf, then the edge can be put in contact with the water, which, by capillary action, spreads up and through the sward. It will soak up quite an amount of water during hot summer weather, and so care will be needed to ensure that the pool is regularly filled up. Where this is successful, another problem sometimes follows: vigorous uncontrolled growth, especially of grass roots that dangle down into the pond.

This can be overcome by using a specially selected turf that will grow on rockwool. This is an inert material widely used for soil-less plant culture, and when used as a pool edging it is neat, clean cut, and very successful in containing the spread of root growth.

Above: *Grass can rapidly grow out of control and create maintenance problems by invading the pond margins.*

1 The use of good quality turf, especially of non-rhizomatous grasses, along with rockwool, can ensure a permanently tidy edge to the pond.

4 Lay the new turf on the dampened rockwool, ensuring a neat edge at the poolside.

2 Lift and remove the matted roots of overgrown turf. Cut back to 30 cm (12 in) beyond the edge. Excavate so that the rockwool can be inserted.

3 Ensure that the new turf can be laid on the rockwool and then water it thoroughly.

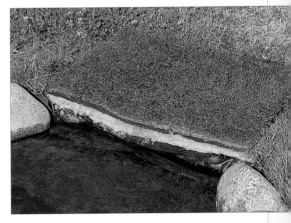

5 Water the turf thoroughly. You must do this regularly until the turf and rockwool knit together. This usually takes a month or more. An occasional weak liquid feed is invaluable.

6 The rockwool will act as a sponge if in contact with the water. When the turf does not touch the water, weekly watering of the edge is advisable to maintain an attractive green sward.

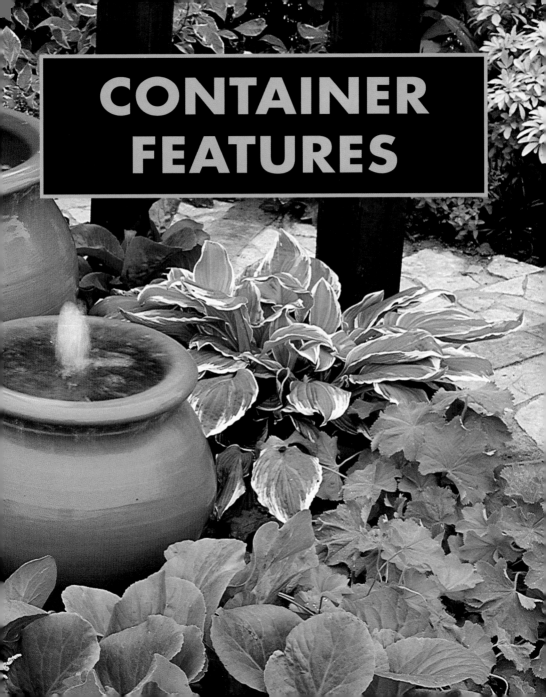

CONTAINER
FEATURES

POSITIONING CONTAINERS

The greatest trend in modern water gardening is the use of containers to create water features. Originally only gardeners who had insufficient space for a pond considered a large bowl or container as suitable for an aquatic endeavor, and then they almost always ended up with a pygmy waterlily, dwarf Japanese reedmace, and solitary goldfish to clear up any mosquito larvae.

Today it is completely different. Of course, many gardeners still love and grow pygmy waterlilies and reedmaces, but container water gardening is very much more about ornamentation and innovation. Nowadays, it has relatively little to do with

Above: *While they are the focus of attention in a small garden, millstone bubblers can also occupy an intimate niche or corner in the broader garden landscape.*

growing aquatic plants in a confined space. Indeed the majority of container water features have no plants and are more likely to be designed to accommodate moving water in some form or other.

The containers that can be used are legion. The current trend is towards selecting a container feature that is either in self-

Tips & handy hints

It is always best to choose the largest container that will look right in the position selected. The greater the volume of water, the less will be the problem of topping up through evaporation. Cooler water also results from a larger volume, and this in turn reduces the occurrence of algal bloom.

Make sure that any container that is to be left out during the winter is frost-proof. In areas where there is severe frost, it is wise to empty all containers during the autumn and provide some kind of cover to prevent rain or snow entering if they are to remain as garden decorations. Otherwise, bring them indoors.

Left: *Oriental water features are usually associated with peace and contemplation. They should be positioned accordingly in the garden.*

assembly kit form, or else integrated with a pre-fitted submersible pump. However, almost any container that will hold water can be used successfully with a little creative thought and enthusiasm.

Positioning containers is quite an art, especially in the broader garden landscape. They should be arranged so that they are small focal points themselves in intimate corners, or positioned where they can be enjoyed in the proximity of seating, whether on a patio or solitary garden bench. All are best enjoyed with the benefit of sunshine, especially those with moving water, beauty and atmosphere being added by shafts of sunlight glistening on the water.

UNADORNED CONTAINERS

*F*or many gardeners, the introduction of a water feature does not mean a traditional planted pool complete with ornamental fish. It implies the use of water for its sound, movement and other special qualities. It may be a pool with a fountain or waterfall, but increasingly people are preferring self-contained water features. These are now available in immense diversity and can bring the magic of moving water to the smallest garden or conservatory.

Not that a garden need be small to accommodate a self-contained water feature, for they are also immensely useful for positioning as focal points in small designed areas and intimate corners. They can be modernistic in appearance, or as traditional as an old hand pump and half a barrel. For

Below and right: *A contrast in styles. The decorated millstone would fit into any traditional garden, while the rotating sphere suggests 21st-century innovation.*

Tips & handy hints

As a self-contained water feature rarely accommodates plants or fish, it can be positioned in either sun or shade. Aesthetically, a sunny spot is better, for then light plays on the fountain spray and brings it to life.

Always position a self-contained water feature that has a reservoir sunk into the ground in a slightly higher position than the surrounding area so that during wet winter weather water does not gather and flood all around it.

Use the deepest reservoir available to reduce the requirement for filling up with water following evaporation. A little pond algaecide added to the water helps to keep the feature, as well as any surrounding pebbles, free from a green algal deposit.

he imaginative water gardener they offer imitless opportunities for innovation.

Self-contained water features are also mostly self-assembled, comprising a sump or eservoir for the submersible pump, the ornamental feature itself, and the option to use pebbles or cobbles as a surround. The majority of self-contained water features pump water over an ornament or artifact. This then flows through a cobble or pebble base that covers the reservoir where the pump is situated and from which the water is re-circulated.

Although most gardeners elect to purchase a ready-made option, those with a practical turn of mind can easily convert an everyday item like a watering can into a flowing water feature, or with a few pieces of bamboo and a rock produce a traditional Japanese deer scarer or *shishi odoshi*.

PLANTED CONTAINERS

For many gardeners, the use of containers for growing aquatics is the only way in which they can enjoy these wonderful plants. For others it presents unique design opportunities, for plant and container combinations can make all manner of statements. A papyrus, Cyperus papyrus, *in an Egyptian style pot, or Japanese iris,* Iris ensata, *in an oriental container are popular examples of such happy and visually appealing combinations.*

These arrangements also bring with them the prospect for gardeners in colder areas of enjoying tropical plants. Protection is provided for the winter months by removing the plants indoors. Where tropical and sub-tropical plants cannot ordinarily be cultivated in the open, container cultivation means that during the late spring and summer the gardener can enjoy the design benefits that a touch of the exotic can bring.

Apart from being grown for their individual beauty, container plants can be grouped together, containers of an appropriate size and configuration being established so that they make neat groups. They can even be arranged so that they are surrounded and united by a decorative edging such as a log roll and create what might be called a 'mobile' garden, individual containers of plants capable of being interchanged at will.

Although conventional watertight pots and planters are the usual choice for cultivating aquatic plants, there is no reason why others cannot be used. A discarded kitchen sink, when dressed with hypertufa, is ideal; so too the tub created from half a barrel. These, along with troughs and window boxes, all make great homes for aquatic and bog garden plants.

Left: *This galvanized trough is enjoying a rewarding new life. Waterlilies flourish in its cool deep water unadorned by any marginal aquatics.*

Tips & handy hints

Select plants that have compatible growth rates and habits when making a mixed planting in the same container. Many aquatic plants, although of modest stature, have quite vigorous root systems and will rapidly swamp weaker neighbours.

Do not try to maintain a natural eco-system, even in a large container. It is best to arrange plants for their visual effect and to accept that changing or filling up with fresh water is a necessary part of maintenance.

Select plants that have attractive foliage for a long period of time, even when they are cultivated principally for their flowers. The quality and condition of the foliage of plants growing in containers is much more obvious than in the tangle of the waterside.

Top left: *The planting around this water feature is what makes it so pleasing to the eye. Try not to neglect a container's immediate surroundings.*

Left: *Growing a pygmy waterlily in a small basket ensures that it can be protected during the winter months.*

PROJECT: A Planted Tub Fountain

The tub fountain is a very effective option for those who want a small moving water feature which is safe for children. It is also one of the easiest to create from standard materials purchased at a garden center.

There are a wide range of tubs available, some of the wooden ones having been used previously to contain other materials. These should be regarded with caution, as the wood might be impregnated with pollutants, in which case internal lining with a piece of pool liner is essential. However, many garden centers now offer wooden tubs which are manufactured for the garden trade, and often these have been waterproofed as well. Of course, there are also tubs made from other materials, and while plastics may not be the first choice in the garden, they should not be completely overlooked.

The selection of a suitable pump must be carefully addressed, for there should be over-capacity to give you the option of turning the flow down to what is required. Never select a pump that will just fulfill the task and no more. This is a false economy.

This tub fountain is ideal for adding a touch of glamour to a terrace or patio.

1 Select a clean watertight tub. Be sure at the time of purchase that the outflow of the pump can be adjusted to ensure the desired flow of water.

2 Choose suitable plants and place them in position. Some height adjustment using bricks under the pots may be necessary.

3 Place a metal grille insert over the pump and thread the plants through carefully. Make sure it is securely positioned, if necessary stapling it in place.

4 Fill the tub to the top with clean, fresh water. You must do this regularly to compensate for water loss through evaporation and fountain splash.

5 Switch on the pump and make any adjustments necessary by regulating the flow adjuster control on the fountain head.

6 Once everything is functioning and the plant arrangement is satisfactory, carefully place paddle stones or cobbles over the mesh support to hide it.

PROJECT: A Barrel and Spout

There are a number of designs incorporating barrels and replica hand pumps available from garden centers. These also have a submersible pump included and built into the structure. Unlike tub fountains which require an outside sump through which to circulate water, the barrel and spout circulate between one another. Occasional splashes as well as evaporation cause some water loss, but this is not significant, although to retain the best visual effect it is sensible continually to observe the water level and to fill it when necessary.

Visually, a barrel and spout combination benefits from the addition of aquatic plants. They make little difference to the ecology of the water body, but frame the structure beautifully if well chosen. There are limits to what can be grown, for the water can be quite turbulent and many aquatic plants, including waterlilies, would suffer badly.

Even the very resilient pondlilies or nuphars would not put up with the turbulence. Floating plants also suffer, so it is principally the more resilient marginals and selected submerged aquatics that can be used.

Above: *Half barrels with hand pumps are very popular self-contained moving water features. They offer an excellent opportunity for growing marginal plants, such as* Alisma plantago-aquatica, Houttuynia cordata *and* Lythrum salicaria *which are used here.*

1 Connect the submersible pump to the outflow pipe in the tub. This is sometimes already attached as an integral feature of the tub when purchased.

2 Fill the tub with clean, fresh water. Switch on the submersible pump and make sure that the flow of water through the pump is satisfactory before adding any plants.

3 Position the plants in the tub. For most marginal aquatic plants, the depth of the water will be too great and so you must raise the containers on bricks. With tub culture it is necessary to confine the plants to small containers, so they will require re-potting annually.

4 It is desirable to have a few submerged plants in the tub, but these will not make a major contribution to water clarity.

5 Although it is not essential to have fish, they are beneficial as they clear up mosquito larvae and other

PROJECT: A Japanese Bog Garden

The Japanese garden is famous for its very meaningful, but minimalist, design. Western cultures are fascinated by the sense of mystique which this conveys, but for the most part find the appearance of pure Japanese garden design and culture a little austere. So it is a popular practice to take a Japanese theme and oriental materials and to fashion them into a western creation which picks out some of the best, and often more colorful, aspects of our own garden culture.

There are a number of manufactured Japanese water garden containers and artifacts which can be established as miniature Japanese landscapes, but it is much more satisfying to create your own. With the ready availability of bamboo in all shapes and sizes from large tubes to ready-made rolls of bamboo matting and screening, it is not difficult to adapt and dress everyday containers and to transform them into something quite special.

With ingenuity, a Japanese themed container can be transformed into a landscape which not only includes water as its focal point, but also draws on the tradition of bonsai, which is especially useful when gardening within the confines of a small yard or on a balcony.

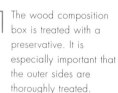

1 The wood composition box is treated with a preservative. It is especially important that the outer sides are thoroughly treated.

2 Insert a piece of pool liner. Make sure that the folds in the corners are bold and simple for ease of fastening.

3 Screw or nail wooden battens, beading, or carpet strip around the top to secure the liner.

4 Dress the outside of the box using fine bamboo matting. This can be purchased from most garden centers. It is cut to size and fastened in position with metal staples.

6 This bonsai specimen adds great character to the scene, but it will not tolerate the wet. Ensure that a solid base is in position to keep the plant clear of the compost. Other ornamentation can then be positioned.

5 Fill the box with compost. For a bog garden, it is best to use a richly organic material. Peat-based potting composts are ideal if mixed with up to 20 percent by volume of garden soil. Arrange the plants so that they have space to develop. Do not disturb the potballs unless they are tightly knotted.

PROJECT: A Bamboo Spout

Although traditional Far Eastern bamboo spouts and *shishi odoshi* (deer scarers) – hinged bamboo spouts that strike a stone when empty, thereby creating a noise to scare away wild animals from crops – were often connected to large established water features, those of the present day which are used to adorn our gardens are generally container water features. With modern technology they are able to stand alone independently of a water garden.

It is common to come across moving bamboo water spouts at the garden center sold as a package, complete with sump and reinforced netting cover, the submersible pump and cobbles included. Indeed, it is the submersible pump which has revolutionized this kind of feature, for it is merely placed in the sump beneath the water which is circulated through the bamboo. Evaporation causes some loss of water, but for the most part it is very efficient and effective.

If you wish to be more innovative than the traditional deer scarer, then it is simple to create your own feature with water tumbling from one cane to the other, providing that the last drop to the cobbles on the ground is immediately over the sump which contains the submersible pump.

1 The pump is positioned in the sump over which the stone bowl is to be placed. The internal load-bearing supports must be sufficiently robust.

2 Place the stone bowl in position so that water will flow from the area of the lip as desired. Tilt it slightly forward to assist this. Place cobbles around the bowl to disguise the sump and to provide secure support for the bowl.

4 Having positioned both supports, take the delivery cane and place it in position on the rests. The hose delivering the water runs up the cane at the back of the spout. Secure the end of the bamboo water spout and insert the delivery hose of the pump. Test once again. Dress with rocks and plants.

3 Position the supports. These are two bamboo canes of equal length bound together with twine or raffia to form a rest.

Plants such as bamboo and ferns are ideal partners for a fountain like this.

5 The completed water spout. It is a charming orientally themed water feature which can become an integral part of a garden landscape or rest easily alone.

PROJECT: A Miniature Marginal Trough

Ceramic bowls and troughs are very attractive propositions for growing marginal aquatic plants, either individually or grouped together in an arrangement. There are also opportunities for grouping such containers together, especially those of varying shapes but the same general design, into more complex arrangements.

Most marginal plants will live happily in bowls and troughs, but marsh marigolds, irises, and the smaller rushes, such as *Juncus effusus* 'Spiralis', have the kind of root systems that will not overwhelm adjacent plants in a trough, nor become tiresome if confined to a bowl. They will require re-potting annually, but will not normally outgrow their positions during a season and look tired and jaded as might more vigorous species, such as *Typha angustifolia*.

When selecting a ceramic bowl, choose one with a good finish which is not going to fade or easily chip or craze. Some are not fully

Above: *The finished planting with water added. This is very shallow and will require regular refilling to counter the effects of evaporation.*

frostproof outdoors during winter weather, and if you select one that is questionable, then it must be removed indoors for the winter. Providing the compost does not dry out, the plants will come to no harm.

Containers often have drainage holes which can be filled with a glass marble held in position by silicone sealant.

2 Place the compost into the container. Use a proper soil-based aquatic planting medium. For marginal and bog garden plants, this should be about 15 cm (6 in) deep.

3 Remove the plants from their pots and plant them firmly. In such a small trough, they are planted directly into the compost.

Iris laevigata
'Variegata'

Zantedeschia aethiopica

Iris laevigata
'Colchesteri'

4 Position the plants and add a layer of gravel to the soil to prevent the water from turning cloudy when it is added. Now top up with water.

PROJECT: A Hypertufa Sink

Although it is most desirable to use a real stone sink or trough for growing aquatic plants, the reality is that they are quite scarce and also expensive to buy. With a little time and ingenuity, a traditional glazed sink can be used and converted into a replica stone vessel by the use of hypertufa. This is an artificial stone-like material which is based upon a naturally occurring stone called tufa. In reality it does not share the same constituents as tufa, but, when well-made, hypertufa can be almost indistinguishable to the naked eye.

Tufa is a porous rock, which in nature is found as a calcareous deposit on the beds of streams or in the vicinity of springs. It is formed underwater and when removed to the garden and dried off, it is used in the cultivation of difficult alpine plants. It is quite a scarce and expensive material, and the original production of hypertufa using sand, cement and peat was intended to produce a cheaper alternative. Indeed it is used to produce tufa-like rocks, but also just as frequently to dress glazed sinks for alpine or miniature water gardening so that they look as if made of natural stone.

Peat

Cement

Sand

1 Hypertufa is made from a mixture of sand, peat, cement, and water. The sand and cement are in equal parts by volume and the peat twice the quantity by volume.

 Aim to make the hypertufa mix quite stiff; too much water leads to a loose mix that is prone to slip.

2 An old glazed sink must have its surface roughened up with a cold chisel before an adhesive can be applied and the hypertufa mixture added.

3 Apply the hypertufa mixture with a small trowel. When mixing, periodically test the moisture content to ensure that it sticks. If too wet or too dry, it may slip off.

4 When the hypertufa is dry, cover the floor of the sink with well-washed pea gravel. Not only does this disguise the bottom, but it catches much of the fine waterborne natural debris.

6 Position the plants carefully in their small containers. The plants should be re-potted annually in aquatic planting compost.

5 To make sure that the water is absolutely clear and to prevent any disturbance of the gravel, pour the water on to a piece of polythene. This disperses the water evenly and smoothly.

PROJECT: A Millstone and Cobble Fountain

Millstones are wonderful for making safe moving water features. Once positioned over a sump, surrounded by cobbles and tastefully planted, one could argue that they have achieved an even more elevated status than was originally envisaged for them when they milled corn.

Real millstones that have ground flour are not easy to come by, but nowadays a wide array is commercially available in varying sizes comprising those made from reconstituted stone, concrete, as well as fiberglass. The reconstituted stone millstones are generally the more pleasing in appearance, and once water has flowed over them for a month or two, they take on a weathered appearance and start to develop a green algal flush.

The most important visual aspect with a millstone feature is to ensure a sufficient flow of water to produce an even spread across a level stone. This may result from a gentle film produced by a strong, silent flow, or a bubbling and tumbling from the center of the stone. Either way it is important that the pump selected for the feature is sufficiently powerful to deliver the quantity of water where it is required in an unfettered flow.

Below: *A bubbling millstone provides a satisfying focal point in a garden setting. Remember to keep the sump topped up with water so that the pump does not run dry.*

1 Measure the sump accurately. By using two canes and a string, the dimensions can be transferred to the ground. Remove the turf to slightly more than the exact circumference of the sump and dig down to the required depth. Level the sump and then secure and support it with pea gravel backfilled between the sump walls and the ground.

2 Position the pump in the center of the sump and arrange the cable so that it does not show, ideally by burying it. Place the top on the sump and run the cable through the small hand hole that is let into the lid. Then adjust the pump so that the outlet is central with the hole so that the water will pass through the millstone accurately.

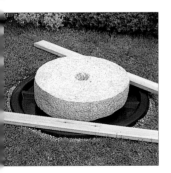

3 Position the millstone. This is achieved more easily with the use of two pieces of stout timber. It can be slid into position supported by these, so reducing the risk of trapped fingers. Fill the sump with water.

4 Once the millstone is in position and level, the area above the sump can be decoratively cobbled.

PROJECT: A Pot Bubbler

Not all water features demand plants or fish;
indeed, the smaller ones are better without
them, especially if the water is intended to
flow. Such fountains are very versatile, not
only being utilized as features in the
garden, but also in the conservatory and
occasionally the home as well.

Selection of the correct pump is vital.
With most contained water features, the
capacity of the pump should be larger than
is required to move the volume of water
intended, and this holds true for the smaller
containers. However, it is conversely also
important that the pump can either be turned
down, or is sufficiently small that in a confined
space it can produce the effect desired rather
than dowsing the surrounding area with
unwanted water. Nowadays there are some
very powerful miniaturized pumps available,
so check their flow rates carefully.

Small water features of this nature are
essentially for summer enjoyment outdoors; they
can be utilized in the conservatory all the year
around, but when used in the garden they must
be taken indoors as autumn approaches and
not set up again outside until late spring when
the risk of frosts has passed.

 *Make sure that any drainage holes
are sealed with silicone sealant – a
fountain like this must be watertight.*

Above: *A simple but very classy contained water feature.*

1 The pump cable is taken through the drainage
hole of the pot and the cavity sealed with
waterproof adhesive. The pot is raised on feet
to allow the wire to pass beneath.

2 The pump is placed in position in the center of the pot. Modern submersible pumps are ideal for restricted conditions and are easily adjusted to provide an accurate water flow. At this point, test the flow of the pump.

3 Measure the depth of the pot so that an accurate assessment can be made of the dimensions required for the wire support.

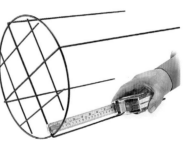

4 Various supports can be used, but the most useful is a standard wire plant support for the herbaceous border with its legs reduced in length. These can be easily removed with wire cutters or bolt croppers.

5 The support is placed in the pot with the outfall of the pump emerging from the center. There should be sufficient room to the rim of the pot to allow for the cobbles.

6 A piece of fine plastic garden netting is cut to the shape of the bowl and rested over the support. This is intended to prevent any fine debris or stones from getting into the water. Dirty water is not only unpleasant, but blocks the filter and sometimes the jet of the fountain as well.

7 Clean cobbles are placed evenly in a mound around the fountain jet. This disguises the netting and permits water to flow back for re-circulation.

PROJECT: A Pot Pool For Marginals

One of the most attractive contained water features is the miniature pool in a pot or bowl. This can be successfully established outside in the garden, although it is often thought more suited to the conservatory. For management purposes it is best stood outdoors, for the water remains cooler and the plants grow more in character in the open air.

Some very interesting pygmy plants can be grown in a confined space, but good management is vital if it is to be a success. Remember that it is important to attend to the feature very regularly, almost daily if it is to remain in pristine condition. A few days of neglect will cause water quality to deteriorate. When this happens with such a small volume of water, it can have disastrous implications for both plants and fish.

Not that fish are essential, for the pot pool can exist perfectly well without, and with such a small amount of water there is little opportunity of striking a natural balance. However, a solitary goldfish can perform a most valuable task in such a water feature, for it is the most efficient and biologically friendly way of controlling the inevitable mosquito larvae that will find their way into the water.

Above: *Here floating candles and flower heads of asters combine with the delicate blooms of* Nymphaea pygmaea *'Helvola'.*

1 The base of the pot can be covered with cobbles to the required depth. These will bring the small container-grown plants to the right level, 5-8 cm (2-3 in) below the rim of the pot. The cobbles will also be effective in trapping debris, which can be periodically and easily siphoned out. The water in a pot pool will require regular replacement.

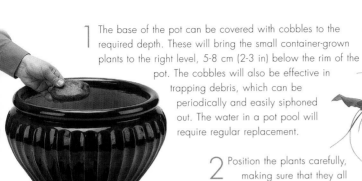

2 Position the plants carefully, making sure that they all stand securely. Choose plants that are happy in the same depth of water and with varying periods of interest.

3 Add water without disturbing the plants. Filling with water because of evaporation will be a regular occurrence and periodic siphoning may be necessary if the water turns green.

4 The completed planting makes an attractive feature for terrace, patio or balcony. A similar arrangement can be contrived for indoors if the plants are suitable.

Tall arum lilies, iris and cottongrass work well in this nicely rounded glazed pot.

PROJECT: A Sunken Container

Not all container water gardens need to be sited above the ground. There is no reason why one should not be sunk into it. Sinking a container presents the opportunity of utilizing unsightly but functional containers which you would not normally consider. It also provides much easier opportunities for creating hidden reservoirs of water from which a pump can operate. Sinking the container also protects the inhabitants from harsh winter weather and in some circumstances permits fish to overwinter outdoors successfully.

When sinking a container it is important to ensure that it is well supported by the surrounding soil. Apart from ensuring stability, it is also as important with a contained water garden to guarantee that it is level from side to side and end to end so that there is no undesirable overflow.

Sunken containers are rather like conventional pools, and so all the precautions that are taken when creating a garden pool should be observed. However, although many of the rules of the pool follow here, because the volume of water used is so small, there is no prospect of plants being arranged so that the water body can maintain a natural ecological balance. Evaporation and rapid temperature changes prevent this.

1 A simple storage container can be utilized to create a most effective pool when sunk into the ground.

2 Make sure that the container is level from side to side and end to end. Backfill firmly and create a level area around.

3 Make a sand and cement mortar mix and trowel it around the top of the container to provide a bed for tiling edges.

4 Lay the tiles evenly around the container, making sure that there is a slight overhang which will disguise the edge. Ensure that they are level.

5 Place the plants into the pool before filling it with water. Only use dwarf varieties in a small container such as this.

A small pool can still provide a home for plants such as dwarf waterlilies, cottongrass, miniature rushes and watermint.

6 The completed pool will require regular maintenance, as the volume of water is too small to sustain a natural balance.

Left: *This sunken pool uses aquatic plants to create a balanced and harmonious feature. If you prefer a more lively effect, it is easy to position a small submersible pump to create a fountain or small water cascade.*

PROJECT: A Brimming Bucket Fountain

Providing that a container will hold water securely or there is a conduit for water to flow through an artifact, an opportunity exists for creating a contained water feature. Your main concern should be to check that it has not contained any pollutant and is made of a material that is unlikely to give rise to maintenance problems.

Wooden containers present the greatest hazard, as they may have previously carried an oil- or tar-based product or been treated with a harmful wood preservative. Copper is unpleasant when fish are around, even short lengths of copper pipe being capable of producing toxicity which can kill goldfish in a rapid and most unpleasant manner when water circulates continually around them.

Surprisingly, lead produces no problems, and neither does galvanized iron nor aluminium. Terracotta is fine, but check that it is frostproof. The same applies to glazed pots and bowls. Plastics and fiberglass present no difficulties, although aesthetically they are much less pleasing. Providing the vessels to be used are solid and watertight, and there is no danger of water pollution, then the scope for innovation is only limited by the creativity of your imagination.

1 Arrange for a standpipe which is disconnected from a mains water supply to be positioned as a water feature, and use bricks or pavers to make a base through which a cable and outlet pipe can be fed.

2 Thread the pump cable through the pot along wi the outlet pipe. Secure th with a waterproof adhesive and allow to dr This provides the sump fc the feature.

3 Position the pot so that the cable and outlet pipe can be passed beneath or between the pavers without pinching it. Make a simple connection to the base of the standpipe using standard connectors.

4 Place the circular support wires on the top of the pot or just within the rim. It may be necessary to trim hem to size with wire cutters. Specially manufactured upports for container features are also available.

Right: *Discarded garden artifacts brought to life as a water feature.*

5 Place the bucket in position under the spout of the watering can. Run a test to make sure that the bucket catches the water and that it flows evenly over the rim. Adjust the level beneath the bucket as necessary.

6 Dress the surface of the support wire with paddle stones. These are very attractive and easier to arrange than cobbles on such a restricted space.

PROJECT: A Timber Lined Pool

Timber containers are greatly under-utilized as far as water gardening is concerned. This is a great shame, as timber is a very versatile material which can be used to construct any plain-sided shape imaginable. It then merely requires lining with pool liner in order to make it watertight and serviceable. There are many methods of applying decoration to the outside and a multitude of types of cladding material that can be used, although most gardeners will agree that the rustic look is generally most appealing.

Timber containers are normally easily moveable, which is a virtue when cleaning out is required, and they are usually visually amenable to being grouped with other containers. In some cases wooden structures can be placed together and then united to form a larger and more complex unit where water circulates from one to the other.

Containers of timber construction look a little stark unplanted. As they are lined, there is always the prospect of the liner being visible,

Above: Here a canna, Iris laevigata and pickerel – Pontederia cordata – have been introduced. They will be able to tolerate the water movement caused by the fountain.

although if properly installed this is not a seriou problem. Any lined water feature is better for being dressed with attractive aquatic plants, as

1 The lined wooden container pictured on page 127 is here given a makeover by the addition of tongue-and-groove wooden facing.

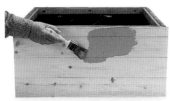

2 The outside of the container is painted with a suitable weatherproof paint. Two or three coats may be required to provide a quality effect.

3 Fill the container with water and prepare for the introduction of a pump to create a moving water feature. Do not fill beyond the top of the liner level.

4 Select a piece of dried tree root as the main focal point for the moving water. Secure the pump hose in position with waterproof silicone sealant.

5 Secure the other end of the clear hose to a small submersible pump which will sit in the container. All joints must be watertight.

6 Place the pump into the water so that the outflow pipe is disguised. Test and adjust the pump to ensure that the flow of water is adequate.

7 Add the plants and, where necessary, adjust their level with stones or a brick. Only marginals and floating aquatics are suitable for this feature.

PROJECT: Ali Baba Fountain

It you really want to be classy, then you can go for a mystical eastern look or a warm Mediterranean effect with an Ali Baba fountain. Tall jars and pots imported from abroad make wonderful features in a western garden.

When selecting a suitable pot for such a feature, its outer appearance is vital. It must have strong color and presence, yet be able to accommodate the necessary tubing to permit the establishment of sufficient water flow to create the desired effect. There can be a considerable lift for a pump, depending upon where it is placed, and it is essential that the capacity, together with the lift and flow required, is carefully considered before the pump is purchased. An excess of capacity is desirable.

Ali Baba fountains are not year-round features in colder climates, for few of the large pots that are available to the home gardener are sufficiently frostproof to tolerate freezing when full of water without shaling, flaking or fracturing. As winter approaches, drain off the water and seal

Above: *A gently weeping Ali Baba fountain is wonderful for creating a mood of garden tranquillity.*

the top to prevent snow and rain entering if you wish to leave the pot outside. Otherwise, take it indoors for protection.

1 As the central flow of water must be accurately controlled, the pump outlet must be secured to a fixed copper pipe.

2 Bricks put into the base of the pot hold the copper pipe in position. The pipe must be central in the jar so that the bubble of water appears in the middle.

3 The submersible pump is placed in the sump prior to the top being replaced and the jar positioned. The electrical cable is disguised as much as possible.

4 Feed the hose from the pump through the base of the jar and connect it to the copper pipe. Seal the hole in the base with a waterproof sealer, as the container must be watertight.

5 Finally, position the jar ensuring that the rim is level to ensure an even overflow. Dress around the base and disguise the sump with fine cobbles.

PROJECT: A Water Staircase

The water staircase is a traditional way of moving water down a slope. In its original form it appeared literally as a staircase over which water flowed. The even spacing and

rises of the stairs ensured one of the most reliable methods of guaranteeing even water dispersal. Nowadays, it loosely embraces other acutely angled falls from one vessel to another in which the drops give the appearance of steps.

An alternative arrangement involves drainpipes that are inserted into a slope to create a step-like arrangement. This produces a similar effect to the traditional staircase, but as the pipes are rounded, the water jumps from one to another in a slightly livelier configuration and the water takes on a more silvery look.

Many water staircases are an integral part of a larger and more traditional garden pool arrangement, but with a little ingenuity they can be used in a more confined space without losing any of their charm, although slightly compromising their grandeur. Not that this need be a problem, for by adapting the original concept to something more modest, a smaller arrangement can achieve an alternative and more appropriate ambience for the modern garden.

1 Cut a groove in the back of the lower sink to accommodate the outflow tube, which takes the water from it to the upper one. Mak sure that the tube and pump connection will f properly and that they can be disguised wher the sinks are placed together.

2 The front of the hypertufa sink can be decorated with paddle stones. These are inserted directly into the we hypertufa and then allowed to dry before the slate spillway is attached. Cut a groove out of the hypertufa and the edge of the sink to accommodate the slate spillway. Use a liberal quantity of strong waterproof adhesive to secure it into position.

3 Place the slate spillway so that it overhangs the edge of the sink. The intention should be to establish an unimpeded curtain of water. The edge of the slate should be smooth and the slate level from side to side.

4 To disguise the outlet pipe of the pump, drill a hole in a similar sized piece of slate and, using the same adhesive, stick it to the back of the upper sink so that the tube will discharge water unobtrusively.

5 Take another piece of slate the same size as the top spillway to create a fake spillway on the lower sink. This disguises the remainder of the pipe and serves as a visual complement to the other slate spillways.

Right: *Two connected sinks with overflows make a water staircase in miniature.*

6 Plants are added. Here a single *Cyperus* is set in the water, but the feature is ringed with plants to soften its outline. These do not detract from the beauty of moving water.

149

PROJECT: A Pygmy Waterlily Pool

Pygmy waterlilies are wonderful indoor plants. Although the majority are completely hardy, they adapt well to sub-tropical conditions and are completely at home in a small bowl in the conservatory or living room. Grown alone, there are few more attractive decorative aquatic plants than pygmy waterlilies.

All are of easy cultivation, requiring a generous layer of aquatic planting compost to be spread on the bottom of the pot and a liberal sprinkling of well-washed pea gravel added over the surface to prevent any escape of the compost into the water.

Water is then poured in, and during the growing season it should be regularly refilled to maintain a level near the rim of the pot. Apart from occasionally removing any filamentous algae that seek to become established, and the regular dead-heading and de-leafing of faded blossoms and foliage, the pot-grown pygmy waterlily is almost entirely self-sustaining.

All the dwarf and pygmy waterlilies are summer-flowering. As autumn approaches and their foliage

naturally fades, water can be removed and the plants dried off. Providing that the compost does not dry out completely, when water is added the following spring they will return to life, although it is wise to replace their compost annually.

Below: *A pygmy waterlily makes a wonderful centerpiece for a decorative bowl. When grown indoors, such waterlilies blossom freely for most of the summer. This plant is Nymphaea pygmaea 'Helvola', a beautiful canary-yellow-flowered variety with dark olive-green leaves which are splashed and stained with maroon and chocolate.*

1 Aquatic planting compost should be spread directly on the bottom of the bowl. As much as one third of the depth of the bowl can be filled with compost.

2 Take the waterlily and plant it in the compost in the center of the bowl with just the nose of the crown above compost level. Water the compost in the bowl thoroughly.

3 Cover the surface of the compost evenly with a thin layer of well-washed pea shingle. This helps to prevent compost escaping and discoloring the water.

4 Add water, taking care not to disturb the gravel. Pour it gently onto a square of polythene. Arrange the waterlily foliage evenly over the surface of the water.

PROJECT: An Indoor Aquatic Plant Display

One of the best ways of growing tropical and sub-tropical aquatic and marginal plants is in decorative pots indoors. While theoretically they should grow best in a traditional lattice-work aquatic planting basket in aquatic compost, this is only the case in a warm tropical or sub-tropical climate when they are out in the open.

In a conservatory or outdoor room, the conditions are not always conducive to successful growth in static water features, owing to varying qualities of light and temperature. When plants are grown in pots, however, they can be easily moved around to take advantage of suitable conditions.

Marginal aquatics are particularly well suited to being grown individually in pots, and once well established, they make a striking feature. Carefully select the pot – it must both be of sufficient size to accommodate the plant, and of an appearance that complements it.

Whatever arrangement is decided, all tropical and sub-tropical marginal plants should be grown in an aquatic planting compost and set sufficiently low in the pot so that a couple of centimeters of water can be maintained over the surface of the compost.

Below: *Fine examples of sub-tropical marginal aquatics that adapt readily to container cultivation. From left to right: Zantedeschia hybrid, Cyperus papyrus and Canna hybrid.*

1 There are many decorative pots that are suitable for the cultivation of aquatics. Most have drainage holes which require sealing. The simplest method to make a pot watertight is to use a waterproof sealant and a marble to block the hole.

2 Place a generous layer of aquatic planting compost into the bottom of the pot. The new plant will root strongly into this.

4 Once further compost has been added and firmed down, top-dress the surface with a layer of well-washed pea shingle.

Add water, soaking the compost. When potting is complete, the plant should be standing in several centimeters of water.

3 Remove the plant from its pot – this is *Cyperus papyrus* – and position it. Ensure that the top of the rootball is several centimeters below the top of the pot to allow for the addition of water.

THE LIVING ENVIRONMENT

A World of Plants and Fish

*A*lthough a water feature is an attractive addition to the garden, it is also a functioning eco-system. How well it works depends very much upon the volume and surface area of the water. Smaller bodies of water rarely have the opportunity to develop any meaningful biological interactions owing to the rapid temperature changes to which they are usually subjected, but larger areas of water can be encouraged to evolve a sustainable ecological balance.

Most garden ponds with dimensions of 2 m x 1.3 m (6 ft x 4 ft) are capable of sustaining a natural balance. A happy association of plants, fish and other aquatic life functions rather like an underwater world one where the submerged plants produce oxygen that helps to sustain fish and other aquatic life and provide sanctuary for aquatic creatures upon which the fish feed, the fish providing nutrients that fertilize the plants.

To achieve this, plants and fish have to be introduced in numbers that complement one another. Snails and freshwater mussels

Below: *One of the great joys of a garden pond is feeding the fish. Feed no more at any one time than the fish can clear up in 20 minutes.*

Above: *The ultimate goal – a small pond where the plants and fish are living in perfect harmony.*

Below: *Ornamental fish bring a pond to life. They also prey on aquatic insect pests and mosquito larvae.*

Tips & handy hints

To ensure a balanced pond, it is essential to establish a generous population of submerged plants. These use the excess nutrients in the water which would otherwise fuel the development of green algae. Work out the surface area of the deeper part of the pond and for every 0.1 sq m (1 sq ft), establish a single bunch of submerged plants.

It is important to provide sufficient shade beneath the water to impede the growth of algae and yet permit the healthy development of the submerged aquatics. Waterlily foliage and that of other deep-water and floating plants should cover up to one third of the surface area of the pond.

can be added as further ingredients in bringing about a balanced environment, one which for the greater part of the year should remain fresh and clean and a sanctuary for myriad aquatic fauna.

Only during the early days of spring, when the sun starts to warm the water, is there likely to be a hiatus, green water-discolouring algae creating a temporary pea-soup-like effect. Once the submerged plants break into growth and mop up the excess nutrients that were sustaining the algae, the water should become clear once again.

PROJECT: Choosing Plants For The Pond

It is always preferable to choose aquatic plants from a specialist nurseryman, or alternatively from a garden center which has an aquatic plant department which is stocked by a specialist grower. Ideally, all marginal plants and waterlilies should be pot grown. Never purchase waterlilies or other aquatic plants which are floating loosely around in a sales tank. They will already have started to deteriorate. Bare-rooted aquatic plants are only satisfactory if received freshly lifted from the nursery.

Some garden centers and pet stores offer pre-packed aquatics, particularly submerged and floating plants. If these are sealed in polythene and hung on a peg board, give them a wide berth. They heat up quickly and spoil.

This also happens sometimes with submerged aquatics which are stocked loose in bunches in a tank. To check whether submerged plants are likely to be a good buy, look at the lead weight around the base of the bunch of cuttings. Black marks on the stems in the vicinity of the foliage indicates that the plant has been bunched for at least a week and that the lead strip is probably causing the stems to rot at the point where they are held together. Such plants should be avoided.

1 Bog garden plants should be well clothed with unblemished foliage.

Hosta

Astilbe

Stipa

4 Plants should be established in their pots and not starved.

2 This hosta represents good value. When removed from the pot, it will be readily divisible.

3 A well-grown plant should display healthy foliage and also be capable of flowering successfully.

Above: *These plants show good husbandry. They are all growing healthily with no signs of pests and diseases. The containers are clean and topped off with a fresh layer of gravel, and all are of reliable varieties.*

Iris

Lobelia

Right: *All the qualities of a good plant are visible here – healthy foliage, a full-sized flower, and well presented container topped with gravel.*

Left: *A plant to avoid – starved and in an inadequate container competing with a mass of seedling weeds.*

Lysimachia

5 It is important that plants are free from pests and display only healthy, undamaged foliage.

PROJECT: Selecting Soils and Compost

The soil or compost that is used for growing pond plants not only has a considerable influence upon their growth and performance, but also upon the clarity of the water in the pond. Healthy aquatic plants require a balance of nutrients in order to prosper, but these have to be available in such a form that the plants can readily assimilate them, without any leaching into the water. When nutrients become freely available in the water, they can be easily used by submerged plants, and when in excess, by green water-discoloring algae too. The successful balance of a water garden depends upon the aquatic plants having a suitable medium in which to grow whereby there are sufficient nutrients available for their well-being, but not for the undesirable lower forms of plant life, like slimes and algae, to prosper.

Aquatic planting composts are the most expensive growing mediums, but they do have the advantage of being balanced for successful pond plant cultivation, the nutrients being available in a slow-release form which does not readily disperse into the water. However, good clear garden soil, especially if of a medium or heavy nature, can be converted into a suitable growing medium for all aquatic plants.

Good clean garden soil is a viable alternative to aquatic planting compost. Any medium to heavy soil is suitable providing that it has not been dressed recently with artificial fertilizer. Sieve it well to remove any sticks and stones or water-polluting organic material.

 Don't ignore the soil that you intend to use for planting aquatic plants. A balanced pond environment and healthy plants result from the use of properly prepared growing medium. You should aim to provide sufficient nutrients for the plants without encouraging green algal bloom.

1 Take some heavy garden soil from a part of the garden which has not recently received fertilizer. Dry thoroughly and break it down so that it can be spooned into an empty jar. Fill to within 2.5 cm (1 in) of the top.

2 Fill the jar to the top with clean tap water, allowing the dry soil particles to soak it up thoroughly. There will be considerable bubbling as the water drives out the air between the crumbs of soil.

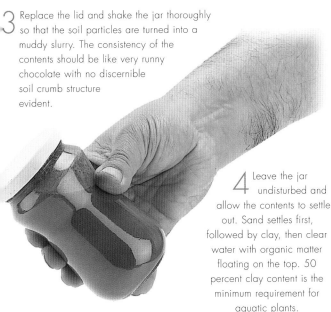

3 Replace the lid and shake the jar thoroughly so that the soil particles are turned into a muddy slurry. The consistency of the contents should be like very runny chocolate with no discernible soil crumb structure evident.

4 Leave the jar undisturbed and allow the contents to settle out. Sand settles first, followed by clay, then clear water with organic matter floating on the top. 50 percent clay content is the minimum requirement for aquatic plants.

PROJECT: Planting in Containers

It is important that pond plants have sufficient opportunity to develop a good root system without becoming over-crowded. Of all the plants that are grown in the decorative garden, aquatic plants unquestionably have the lustiest root growth. For this reason they are best grown in containers where they can be prevented from straying into one another, a particular benefit when routine division of the rootstocks takes place.

Aquatic plants are unlike other garden plants, for they do not grow well in ordinary plant pots. It is true that plants will prosper for a short time, but before the end of the season they will go into decline, irrespective of the compost. The roots of the plants must be able to escape into the water and for the compost to be effectively ventilated by direct exposure to the water through the sides of a lattice-work basket. In a closed pot, within 12 to 18 months the compost will turn blue or black and smell very unpleasant.

There are a wide range of aquatic planting baskets available, and although they are more expensive than pots or similar containers, they are an excellent investment and ensure that pond plants develop to their full potential.

Planting containers range from micromesh and traditional lattice-work and burlap arrangements to fabric planting bags.

1 Prepared soil or aquatic planting compost is put into the basket. Those with wide mesh sides should be lined with burlap to prevent soil spillage.

2 Prepare the plant by removing at least three-quarters of the foliage. Shorten back the root growth. A plant which is disturbed during its growing season dies back anyway, so removing excess growth works to its advantage and ensures rapid re-establishment.

3 For marginal aquatics, multiple plantings are to be prepared, with three or four plants to each basket. Firm the plants in well and top up with compost as necessary. An initial watering settles the compost and drives out any

4 Top off the planting with a generous layer of well-washed pea gravel. This prevents soil spillage and fish disturbance.

5 With planting complete, surplus burlap from the lining of the basket should be trimmed off neatly with a pair of scissors.

6 The completed planting should be thoroughly watered before being placed in position in the pond. This drives out all the air and settles the compost.

PROJECT: Making Natural Planting

There are occasions when planting directly into the pool is desirable. This is mostly when the pool has a natural soil bottom, or alternatively there is a liner sandwiched between the excavated shape and a generous layer of soil. In both cases the control of the spread of the plants has to be by soil sculpting. This involves varying the internal levels of the pool so that only plants of certain kinds can grow. For example, if there is a shallow area of water 15 cm (6 in) deep where typha is flourishing, and the pool profile suddenly drops to 60 cm (24 in), the typha becomes restricted as it cannot survive in a 60-cm (24-in) depth of water. Thus, the edge of the planting and its ultimate shape can be determined by the line of excavation between the 15-cm (6-in) and 60-cm (24-in) depths. The growth of the typha follows the area where the depth falls away.

It is quite possible to push bare-rooted plants into the mud on the floor of a naturally lined pool and for them to quickly establish. However, a much better start is achieved if initial plantings are made with an aquatic planting compost or prepared soil, the plants being wrapped in a textile which slowly deteriorates, but from which their roots can escape.

Take care with free-growing plants, such as reeds and rushes. You will need to check their invasive habit.

PLANTING IN BURLAP

1 Planting in an earth-bottomed pool can be assisted by the use of burlap wraps. Take a bare-rooted plant, add aquatic planting compost, and place on a burlap square.

2 Wrap the rootball up, securing it like a small parcel. Soak it thoroughly in water to drive out the air before lowering it into its permanent position in the pond.

3 Plants planted in burlap wraps are a perfect solution for the earth-bottomed pool. The roots penetrate the burlap and establish quickly into surrounding soil. Within a couple of seasons the burlap rots away without having impaired the development of the plants.

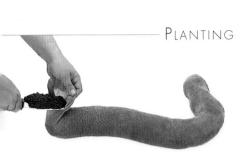

1 Where a natural-looking controlled planting is required, soil rolls made from old stockings or tights can be utilized. Fill the detached legs with a suitable compost.

2 Prepare plants of vigorous marginal aquatics for planting. Make small holes in the fabric, just sufficient to permit the roots to be pushed through and into the compost. Plant several plants of the same species in the roll.

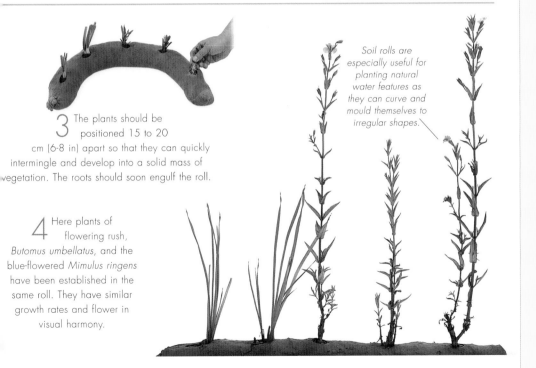

3 The plants should be positioned 15 to 20 cm (6-8 in) apart so that they can quickly intermingle and develop into a solid mass of vegetation. The roots should soon engulf the roll.

4 Here plants of flowering rush, *Butomus umbellatus*, and the blue-flowered *Mimulus ringens* have been established in the same roll. They have similar growth rates and flower in visual harmony.

Soil rolls are especially useful for planting natural water features as they can curve and mould themselves to irregular shapes.

PROJECT: Planting a Waterlily

Waterlilies are not only the most decorative and important aquatic plants, but also the longest-lived and most expensive acquisitions for the pool. When purchasing a waterlily the cost is likely to be as much as a young decorative garden tree and the prospect of longevity much the same, although a waterlily does require regularly dividing.

The growth of every plant reflects the soil in which it is growing, and for waterlilies this is particularly true, for they are gross feeders. This demand for nutrient used to be met by the liberal use of well-rotted animal manure or decomposing turf and many old gardening books made this recommendation. The problem with this was that although the waterlilies prospered, so too did the various slimes and algaes which unfortunately discolor pond water.

Waterlilies are now widely sold growing in containers, and often these can be introduced directly to the pool where they will grow away for a season without requiring any attention. Even if they require immediate re-potting, container-grown waterlilies are still the best option for the newcomer to water gardening, and by using a balanced planting compost, the requirements of the plants and the continued clarity of the water are both addressed.

 By cutting off the old fibrous roots, fresh growth is stimulated which will make rapid and unimpeded progress.

1 Select a strong-growing crown from a clump of waterlilies and remove any old or dying root system. As most waterlilies grow, they push out new creeping root systems, and the starchy remains of the old are of no further value. Remove all surplus fibrous root growth to within about 1 cm (0.4 in) of the crown of the plant.

2 All surface foliage and developing flower buds should be removed, the stems being cut back close to the main crown. If allowed to remain, the majority of surface floating foliage will in any event become yellow and die.

3 The ideal waterlily crown should consist of a solid portion of starchy root system with a strong growing point with vigorous spear-like underwater shoots. Embryo flower buds can remain, as these may develop into blossoms.

4 Prepare a large planting basket with a suitable growing medium, and plant the waterlily firmly in the center. Water the compost to drive out the air.

5 Top-dress the container with washed pea gravel to reduce soil spillage and disturbance by fish once it is placed into the pool. Water the container again thoroughly.

6 Newly planted waterlilies can be placed on the floor of the pool in their final positions. They will rapidly establish themselves, producing a mass of fibrous roots and both submerged and floating foliage. Planted before mid-summer, a reasonable show of flowers can be expected in the first season.

Planted waterlilies rapidly develop new foliage.

Flowers generally bloom in high summer.

PROJECT: Fertilizing Plants

Pond plants by their very nature are vigorous growers and heavy feeders. They require fertilizing at least once every season, but this has to be done in such a way that it benefits the plants and does not leach out into the water where it can encourage the development of a green algal bloom. The requirements of the first season after planting can be overcome by selecting a suitable well-balanced aquatic planting compost. Such a compost should contain sufficient nutrients to allow lusty growth for an entire season with no requirement for feeding until early the following summer. Most specialist-manufactured aquatic planting composts are well formulated and provide the likely nutritional requirements necessary for all aquatic plants.

The pool itself will yield nutrients too, both from the inevitable decomposition of aquatic vegetation as well as the deposits from fish. However, in a well-balanced pool, this will be insufficient to sustain the kind of growth and flowering that we expect from decorative pond plants if water clarity is to also be assured. The careful use of selected artificial fertilizers is desirable.

FEEDING PLANTS

All aquatic plants require nourishment, but not all demand formal feeding. Both submerged and floating aquatics derive their nutrients directly from the water, in the case of submerged plants their root systems performing an anchoring role rather than one which yields up nutrients. In the main they are foliar feeders and extract nutrients from the water rather than the growing medium. Thus, in the well-maintained pond where plants and livestock are established in harmony, all the essential nourishment required comes from the water.

Waterlilies, deep-water aquatics and marginal plants, on the other hand, benefit from regular feeding. These derive their nourishment principally from the growing medium. While this should be enriched for the benefit of the plants, it should be done in such a way that there is minimal leaching into the water.

Above: *When fertilizer leaches into the water, slimes and algae become a problem, so keep it contained within the compost adjacent to the roots of the plants.*

1 Take wet clay and mould it into small balls. Add up to 25 percent by volume of bonemeal or fishmeal, rolling the material into the ball.

2 Place the fertilizer pill into the compost next to the plant. Nutrients will be slowly released into the compost without polluting the water.

Right: *Aquatic plant fertilizer is available in small plastic sachets with perforations which permit the absorption of water. The sachet is pressed into the compost next to each plant.*

Above: *There are several pill-like slow-release fertilizers which can be used for aquatic plants in the same way as for shrubs and border subjects.*

Marginals, like this arum lily, will benefit from the application of a slow-release fertilizer.

LARGE AND MEDIUM WATERLILIES

Waterlilies are beautiful plants that look very exotic, suggesting that they may not be easy to cultivate. The reverse is true; they are amongst the simplest aquatics to grow providing that they are established in a heavy soil-based compost and planted in aquatic planting baskets.

As they are usually only lifted and divided in the spring every three or four years, they require regular feeding with an aquatic plant fertilizer. This is best administered as a tablet pushed into the compost beside the plant each spring.

Below: Nymphaea 'Marliacea Chromatella' is one of the oldest yellow-flowered waterlilies, and one of the best.

When planting, always top-dress the compost with a generous layer of pea-shingle. This prevents compost from escaping into the water and deters the fish from causing a disturbance in their quest for aquatic insect life.

Nymphaea 'Charles de Meurville'
Large plum-colored blossoms with petals that are sparingly streaked with white. Large, rounded, olive-green leaves. Spread: 1.2-1.8 m (4-6 ft). Depth: 1.2-1.8 m (4-6 ft).
Flowering period: summer.

Nymphaea 'Escarboucle'
Large richly fragrant crimson blossoms with bright yellow stamens. Fresh green rounded leaves.
Spread: 1.2-1.8 m (4-6 ft).
Depth: 1.2-1.8 m (4-6 ft).
Flowering period: summer.

Nymphaea 'Marliacea Albida'
Fragrant white blossoms up to 15 m (6 in) across. Dark green leaves with purplish undersides.
Spread: 45-90 cm (1.5-3 ft).
Depth: 45-90 cm (1.5-3 ft).
Flowering period: summer.

Nymphaea 'Marliacea Chromatella'
Large canary-yellow blossoms are freely produced. Olive-green foliage splashed and stained with maroon and bronze. Spread: 45-75 cm (1.5-2.5 ft). Depth: 45-75 cm (1.5-2.5 ft).
Flowering period: summer.

Nymphaea 'Mrs. Richmond'
Beautiful pale rose-pink flowers that pass to crimson with age. Mid-green rounded foliage.
Spread: 60-90 cm (2-3 ft).
Depth: 45-75 cm (1.5-2.5 ft).
Flowering period: summer.

Nymphaea 'Pink Sensation'
Bright pink star-like blossoms. Deep-green rounded foliage with reddish undersides.
Spread: 45-75 cm (1.5-2.5 ft).
Depth: 45-75 cm (1.5-2.5 ft).
Flowering period: summer.

Small and Pygmy Waterlilies

*I*n addition to the traditional waterlily of the garden pond, there are many smaller-growing kinds for modest water features and pygmy varieties that grow happily in tubs and containers. All should be planted during late spring or early summer and afforded a sunny position. Those that are to be grown in a pond should be planted in aquatic planting baskets, while waterlilies in tubs or pots are best established directly into the compost.

Waterlilies that are grown in baskets should receive an aquatic fertilizer tablet pushed into the compost close to the plant each spring. They will also require lifting and dividing every three or four years. Pygmy waterlilies growing in containers should be replanted with fresh compost each spring.

Below: *Nymphaea pygmaea 'Alba' is the perfect pygmy waterlily for a sink or tub water garden.*

Winter Maintenance

When pygmy waterlilies that are growing in containers die back in the autumn, empty the container of water. The container can then be removed to a safe place away from severe frost. Providing that the compost is not allowed to dry out, the waterlilies will remain safe until it is time for lifting and replanting next spring.

Nymphaea 'Froebeli'
Crimson blossoms are produced freely amongst rounded to oval dark green foliage.
Spread: 30-75 cm (1-2.5 ft).
Depth: 30-45 cm (1-1.5 ft).
Flowering period: summer.

Nymphaea 'Hermine'
Tulip-like pure white blossoms which open fully to a cup-shape. Dark-green oval leaves.
Spread: 30-60 cm (1-2 ft).
Depth: 45-60 cm (1.5-2 ft).
Flowering period: summer.

Nymphaea 'Laydekeri Purpurata'
Deep vinous-red blossoms. Dark olive-green leaves that are occasionally splashed with purple.
Spread: 45-60 cm (1.5-2 ft).
Depth: 30-45 cm (1-1.5 ft).
Flowering period: summer.

Nymphaea pygmaea 'Alba'
The tiniest white-flowered waterlily, with blossoms no more than 2.5 cm (1 in) across. Dark-green oval leaves. Spread: 20-30 cm (8-12 in).
Depth: up to 30 cm (1 ft).
Flowering period: summer.

Nymphaea pygmaea 'Helvola'
A tiny waterlily with canary yellow flowers and olive-green foliage heavily mottled with purple and brown.
Spread: 20-30 cm (8-12 in).
Depth: up to 30 cm (1 ft).
Flowering period: summer.

Nymphaea 'Sioux'
Pale yellow buds open to orange blossoms that pass to crimson with age. Purplish-green mottled foliage.
Spread: 30-60 cm (1-2 ft).
Depth: 30-45 cm (1-1.5 ft).
Flowering period: summer.

DEEP-WATER AQUATICS

*D*eep-water aquatics are a useful accompaniment to waterlilies, occupying the same part of the pond and often extending the season of floral interest. The majority are of more determined growth and spread than waterlilies and so require more regular rationalizing of surface growth during the summer. Most species require lifting and dividing every second year, although Orontium aquaticum *will be happy for four or five years without disturbance.*

Feeding is important, the regular spring use of aquatic plant fertilizer tablets pushed

Below: *The scented* Aponogeton distachyos *flowers continuously from late spring until the onset of winter.*

into the compost next to the plants being invaluable. All deep-water aquatics prosper in full sun, although both *Nuphar* and *Nymphoides* will cope with a little shade and unlike waterlilies, are tolerant of moving water

Aponogeton distachyos

Deliciously scented forked white blossoms with distinctive black stamens. Oval to oblong green leaves splashed with maroon. Spread: 30-90 cm (1-3 ft). Depth: 30-90 cm (1-3 ft). Flowering period: late spring to winter.

Nuphar advena

Globular yellow blossoms often tinged with purple and with bright coppery-red stamens. Leathery green leaves. Spread: 45 cm-1.5 m (1.5-5 ft). Depth: 30 cm-1.5 m (1-5 ft) Flowering period: summer.

Nuphar lutea

Small bottle-shaped yellow flowers with a distinctive alcoholic aroma. Leathery green leaves. Spread: 60 cm-2.4 m (2-8 ft). Depth: 30 cm-2.4 m (1-8 ft). Flowering period: summer.

Nymphoides peltata

Bright yellow-fringed blossoms produced freely amongst small rounded green leaves that are often splashed with brown. Spread: 30-75 cm (1-2.5 ft). Depth: 30-75 cm (1- 2.5 ft). Flowering period: summer.

Orontium aquaticum

Numerous upright pencil-like bright gold and white blossoms are produced amongst blue-green lance-shaped foliage. Spread: 45-60 cm (1.5-2 ft). Depth: up to 45 cm (1.5 ft) Flowering period: summer.

Polygonum amphibium

Short spikes of deep rosy pink blossoms are borne amongst mid-green, floating lance-shaped foliage. Spread: 45-90 cm (1.5-3 ft). Depth: 30-90 cm (1-3 ft). Flowering period: summer.

MARGINALS

*M*arginal plants contribute little to the ecological balance of a pond, but they do provide decoration and a home for myriad aquatic creatures. They are best planted during late spring or early summer, for then there is the prospect of a reasonable display of flowers during the first season.

Established marginal plants must be fed during the early spring, just as they are breaking into growth. Use an aquatic fertilizer tablet and push it into the compost next to each

Below: *Marginal aquatics in all their glory – Myosotis* scorpioides *is accompanied by the moisture-loving* Ligularia *'Desdemona' and* Primula florindae.

---------------- DIVIDING CALTHAS ----------------

The marsh marigold, *Caltha palustris*, is usually treated slightly differently from other marginal plants when requiring to be lifted and divided. This flowers during the spring, so enjoy the blossoms before lifting and dividing overcrowded plants. Cut back the foliage and roots prior to replanting to ensure rapid re-establishment.

plant. Most marginal plants require lifting and dividing at least every third year. Do this in the early spring, selecting only the youngest and most vigorous portions for replanting. Top-dress freshly planted containers with fine pea gravel

Calla palustris
A creeping plant with glossy
green heart-shaped leaves.
Small white arum-like flowers.
Height: 15-30 cm (6 in-1 ft).
Spread: 15-30 cm (6 in-1 ft).
Flowering period: summer.

Caltha palustris
Mounds of glossy green scalloped
foliage. Bright golden-yellow,
waxy, saucer-shaped blossoms.
Height: 30-60 cm (1-2 ft).
Spread: 30-60 cm (1-2 ft).
Flowering period: spring.

Canna Longwood hybrids
Spikes of handsome, brightly colored
orchid-like blossoms amongst narrow
green spade-like leaves.
Height: 1-1.2 m (3-4 ft).
Spread: 45-60 cm (1.5-2 ft).
Flowering period: summer.

Lysichiton americanus
Large bright-yellow arum-like
flowers are produced before the
bold green cabbagy leaves.
Height: 60-90 cm (2-3 ft).
Spread: 60-75 cm (2-2.5 ft).
Flowering period: spring.

Mentha aquatica
An aromatic scrambling plant
with hairy green foliage. Clusters
of lilac-pink blossoms.
Height: 30-45 cm (1-1.5 ft).
Spread: 30-45 cm (1-1.5 ft).
Flowering period: summer.

Myosotis scorpioides
Tightly arranged heads of small
bright blue flowers. Smooth,
narrow, lance-like leaves.
Height: 20-30 cm (8-12 in).
Spread: 30 cm (1 ft).
Flowering period: summer.

MARGINALS

*A*lthough most marginal plants are best established in containers, there are occasions when this is not practical, especially with natural ponds. If the pond has an earth bottom, then take squares of burlap or burlap, place each plant, together with a quantity of soil, in the center, and tie it up like a parcel. It can then be placed in the water where it will quickly become established and root into the surrounding pond floor.

Apart from regular fertilizing, the routine maintenance of marginal plants is restricted to removing faded flower heads and dead or damaged foliage. A number of marginal plants produce extremely viable seeds, which if allowed to self-sow can produce a major weed problem, so old flower head removal is essential.

—VIGOROUS MARGINALS—

Several of the more vigorous marginal plants that are used for disguising the pond edge, such as *Mentha aquatica* and *Veronica beccabunga*, are best replaced annually from soft stem cuttings taken during the early spring. These root easily in pots of wet soil stood in a bowl in a cold frame.

Right: *The North American pickerel,* Pontederia cordata, *is a reliable summer flowering marginal that makes a fine accompaniment to the flowering rush,* Butomus umbellatus.

Peltandra virginica
Greenish-white arum-like flowers
are produced freely amongst glossy
arrow-like foliage.
Height: 45-60 cm (1.5-2 ft).
Spread: 30-45 cm (1-1.5 ft).
Flowering period: summer.

Pontederia cordata
Spikes of soft blue flowers
appear among glossy, dark, oval
or lance-shaped green leaves.
Height: 60-90 cm (2-3 ft).
Spread: 15-20 cm (6-8 in).
Flowering period: late summer.

Ranunculus lingua 'Grandiflora'
Large, yellow, buttercup-like flowers.
Lance-shaped green leaves are borne
on reddish flushed hollow stems.
Height: 60-90 cm (2-3 ft).
Spread: 45-60 cm (1.5-2 ft).
Flowering period: summer.

Sagittaria sagittifolia
Papery-white blossoms, each with
a prominent purple-black eye.
Distinctive arrow-shaped leaves.
Height: 45-60 cm (1.5-2 ft).
Spread: 20-30 cm (8-12 in).
Flowering period: summer.

Veronica beccabunga
Dark blue flowers with distinctive
white eyes. Scrambling semi-
evergreen foliage.
Height: 15-20 cm (6-8 in).
Spread: 15-20 cm (6-8 in).
Flowering period: summer.

Zantedeschia aethiopica
Pure white arum flowers are
produced above bright green
heart-shaped leaves.
Height: 60-90 cm (2-3 ft).
Spread: 30-45 cm (1-1.5 ft).
Flowering period: summer.

REEDS AND RUSHES

*O*f all the marginal aquatic plants, it is the reeds and rushes which are the best known and loved. However, without proper management they can be a problem. Always grow them in containers so that their root spread is restricted, and place them in a sheltered place so that the wind does not continually turn over the inevitably top-heavy basket.

In a natural soil-bottomed pond their spread can be controlled successfully by soil sculpting. This is the creating of marginal

Below: *The needle-like stems of* Schoenoplectus *are excellent for bringing strong architectural lines to a pool.*

areas where they can spread unhindered, but at the edges there are sheer drops to a depth in which they cannot grow. The edge of the growth is thereby determined by the sweep of the marginal area.

Acorus calamus
Fresh, green, tangerine-scented, sword-like leaves. Small, yellowish, horn-like flowers are freely produced.
Height: 75-90 cm (2.5-3 ft).
Spread: 30-45 cm (1-1.5 ft).
Flowering period: summer.

Butomus umbellatus
Slender, bright-green, glossy, and slightly twisted foliage. Handsome umbels of showy pink flowers.
Height: 60-90 cm (2-3 ft).
Spread: 30-45 cm (1-1.5 ft).
Flowering period: summer.

Carex pendula
A sedge with broad green strap-like leaves and long, drooping, brownish-green, catkin-like flowers.
Height: 90 cm-1.2 m (3-4 ft).
Spread: 45-60 cm (1.5-2 ft).
Flowering period: summer.

Eriophorum angustifolium
An acid-loving rush-like plant with slender dark-green leaves and cotton-wool-like seed heads.
Height: 30-45 cm (1-1.5 ft).
Spread: 15-30 cm (6in-1 ft).
Flowering period: summer.

Schoenoplectus tabernaemontani
'Zebrinus' Upright needle-like stems which are attractively banded alternately with dark green and creamy white.
Height: 90 cm-1.2 m (3-4 ft).
Spread: 45-60 cm (1.5-2 ft).
Flowering period: summer.

Typha minima
Dark-green, slender, grassy foliage amongst which chunky rounded brown fruiting heads are produced.
Height: 30-45 cm (1-1.5 ft).
Spread: 15-20 cm (6-8 in).
Flowering period: summer.

IRISES

There are many different species and varieties of iris that can be grown in the margins of a pond or to decorate a streamside. These are easily managed, especially when grown in planting baskets and a good heavy compost. They require lifting and dividing every three or four years and between times should be fed each spring with a slow-release aquatic fertilizer. Use a tablet or sachet and push one into each container next to the plant each spring.

Irises must have an open sunny position. They are tolerant of both still and moving water and are therefore excellent for stabilizing the banks of a stream. All except *Iris pseudacorus* will also adapt well to life in a tub water garden or a container.

Below: Iris laevigata 'Variegata' has beautiful variegated foliage for much of the year. In mid-summer it produces fine blue blossoms. It is a reliable marginal aquatic for water features of all kinds.

TIME FOR DIVISION

Irises, unlike other marginal plants, are only lifted and divided when flowering is over. As soon as the blossoms fade, remove the plants from their containers, separate them into separate fans of leaves, and cut both the roots and leaves back hard. Replant the most vigorous young plants.

Iris laevigata
Bright blue flowers freely produced amongst sword-like foliage. Many different colored hybrid varieties.
Height: 60-90 cm (2-3 ft).
Spread: 30-45 cm (1-1.5 ft).
Flowering period: summer.

Iris laevigata 'Variegata'
Bright blue flowers and startling green and white sword-like foliage.
Height: 60-75 cm (2-2.5 ft).
Spread: 30-45 cm (1-1.5 ft).
Flowering period: summer.

Iris pseudacorus
Tall mid-green strap-like leaves and bright yellow blossoms with distinctive dark markings. Vigorous.
Height: 90 cm-1.2 m (3-4 ft).
Spread: 45-60 cm (1.5-2 ft).
Flowering period: summer.

Iris pseudacorus 'Golden Queen'
Bright golden-yellow blossoms freely produced amongst the bold, green, sword-like foliage.
Height: 90 cm-1.2 m (3-4 ft).
Spread: 45-60 cm (1.5-2 ft).
Flowering period: summer.

Iris pseudacorus 'Variegata'
A spectacular foliage plant with creamy-yellow and green-striped foliage. Bright yellow flowers.
Height: 60-75 cm (2-2.5 ft).
Spread: 30-45 cm (1-1.5 ft).
Flowering period: summer.

Iris versicolor 'Vernal'
Narrow petalled lilac pink blossoms with white zoning. Bold green sword-like foliage.
Height: 60-75 cm (2-2.5 ft).
Spread: 30-45 cm (1-1.5 ft).
Flowering period: summer.

FLOATING AND SUBMERGED PLANTS

Floating and submerged plants are essential components of the well-balanced pond. The submerged plants mop up an excess of nutrients that encourage the growth of green water-discoloring algae, while the floating plants provide shade that cuts down the amount of light falling directly into the water.

Floating plants are planted by being merely tossed onto the surface of the water. Submerged aquatics, although surviving without planting, are best established in an aquatic planting compost. Most submerged plants are purchased in bunches. When planting, be sure to bury the lead weight that holds the bunch together or else it will rot through and the stems will become detached.

—AVOID MOVING WATER—

While all submerged aquatic plants have some tolerance of moving water, it is ill-advised to place floating aquatics in a small pond with either a fountain or waterfall, as water movement is likely to pile them up at the farthest end. Where there is moving water, depend upon deep-water aquatics for surface shade.

Right: Ranunculus aquatilis *provides the underwater focus in this planted container.*

Hottonia palustris
Submerged plant. White or lilac-flushed blossoms are held above the water. Whorls of bright green filigree foliage.
Depth: up to 60 cm (2 ft).
Flowering period: summer.

Hydrocharis morsus-ranae
Floating plant. Small white three-petalled blossoms are produced freely above clusters of green kidney-shaped foliage.
Spread: 30-45 cm (1-1.5 ft).
Flowering period: summer.

Lagarosiphon major
Submerged plant. Dark-green, crispy, submerged foliage produced in dense finger-like strings. Small, insignificant flowers.
Depth: up to 90 cm (3 ft).
Flowering period: summer.

Ranunculus aquatilis
Submerged plant. Beautiful papery white blossoms with yellow centers. Clover-like floating leaves and finely divided submerged foliage.
Depth: up to 60 cm (2 ft).
Flowering period: summer.

Stratiotes aloides
Floating and submerged plant. Narrow-leafed foliage like a pineapple top. Pinkish-white papery blossoms.
Spread: 30 cm (1 ft).
Flowering period: summer.

Trapa natans
Floating plant. Neat rosettes of dark green rhomboidal floating foliage, amongst which pretty pure-white blossoms are produced.
Spread: 30-45 cm (1-1.5 ft).
Flowering period: summer.

FOLIAGE BOG PLANTS

*I*n the bog garden, the lush growth of foliage plants provides a wonderful complement and foil for the often brightly colored flowers of other bog garden plants. The production of so much foliage takes a considerable amount of nutrients out of the soil. While it is important to replace these each spring with the localized application of a slow-release fertilizer, over-feeding must be resisted so that the plants do not grow out of character, nor fertilizer leach into the adjacent pond.

Below: *The royal fern,* Osmunda regalis, *is one of the finest hardy ferns for the waterside.*

KEEP THEM MOIST

Continuous moisture is essential to all foliage bog garden plants if their leaves are to remain lush and not develop brown edges or patches of die-back. Before growth commences in early spring, apply a generous mulch of well-rotted organic matter to the bog garden to conserve moisture.

Bog garden plants are usually planted during the dormant winter and early spring season, although container-grown plants can be established at any time of the year if kept well watered initially.

Darmera peltata
Domed heads of small pink flowers appear on strong stems in advance of the large umbrella-like leaves.
Height: 75-90 cm (2.5-3 ft).
Spread: 45-60 cm (1.5-2 ft).
Flowering period: spring.

Hosta fortunei 'Aureomarginata'
Large, bright green, gold-margined foliage. Spires of pendent, tubular, lilac to violet blossoms.
Height: 60-90 cm (2-3 ft).
Spread: 30-45 cm (1-1.5 ft).
Flowering period: summer.

Hosta undulata 'Mediovariegata'
Beautiful, slightly twisted cream and green variegated foliage. Spires of tubular lilac flowers.
Height: 30-45 cm (1-1.5 ft).
Spread: 20-30 cm (8-12 in).
Flowering period: summer.

Matteuccia struthiopteris
Bright green lacy fronds arranged like a shuttlecock around a stout woody crown. Dark colored central fertile fronds.
Height: 90 cm (3 ft).
Spread: 45 cm (1.5 ft).

Onoclea sensibilis
Erect, flattened soft green fronds with a pinkish flush are produced by this fern from a black creeping rhizomatous rootstock.
Height: 45-60 cm (1.5-2 ft).
Spread: 20-30 cm (8-12 in).

Osmunda regalis
Bold, tall, leathery, divided fronds which emerge pale green and pass through mid-green to bronze with age.
Height: 1.2-1.8 m (4-6 ft).
Spread: 60-90 cm (2-3 ft).

FLOWERING BOG PLANTS

The bog garden is a wonderful adjunct to the garden pond. Not only does it extend the area of interest and present considerable design opportunities for the gardener, but the plants that grow in marshy places have flowering seasons which often extend beyond that of their truly aquatic cousins.

Plant during the dormant winter and early spring period, preparing the soil thoroughly, ensuring that any perennial weeds are removed. If allowed to remain, they cause endless maintenance problems in such a wet

Below: Primula helodoxa, *glory of the bog, an appropriate name for this hardy and colorful perennial.*

─────── DEADHEADING ───────

To ensure strong plant growth and free-flowering, it is essential to remove faded flower spikes from all bog garden plants. This not only reduces the opportunity for troublesome self-seeding, but also, in the case of primulas and trollius, often encourages some modest, but useful, secondary flowering later in the season.

environment. Incorporate plenty of well-rotted garden compost, for although bog garden plants do not require a rich soil, they do benefit from one that is generously endowed with organic matter.

Astilbe arendsii hybrids
Dense plumes of brightly colored long-lasting blossoms are produced above deeply cut dark-green foliage.
Height: 45-90 cm (1.5-3 ft).
Spread: 25-45 cm (10 in-1.5 ft).
Flowering period: summer.

Filipendula ulmaria
Frothy spires of tiny sweetly scented creamy-white blossoms. Deeply cut mid-green foliage.
Height: 60 cm-1.2 m (2-4 ft).
Spread: 30-60 cm (1-2 ft).
Flowering period: summer.

Iris ensata
Dense tufts of broad grassy foliage. Exotic-looking, brightly colored, broad-petalled blossoms are freely produced.
Height: 60-75 cm (2-2.5 ft).
Spread: 30-45 cm (1-1.5 ft).
Flowering period: summer.

Lobelia cardinalis
Startling bright red blossoms are produced in dense spikes above handsome beetroot-colored foliage.
Height: 60-90 cm (2-3 ft).
Spread: 30-45 cm (1-1.5 ft).
Flowering period: summer.

Primula candelabra hybrids
Tiered whorls of blossoms in a range of creams, reds, orange, purples, and yellow. Coarse cabbagy foliage. Height: 60-75 cm (2-2.5 ft).
Spread: 30-45 cm (1-1.5 ft).
Flowering period: early summer.

Trollius 'Golden Queen'
Large, bright, golden-yellow, globular buttercup-like flowers. Divided dark-green basal foliage.
Height: 45-60 cm (1.5-2 ft).
Spread: 30 cm (1 ft).
Flowering period: early summer.

PROJECT: Stocking A Pond With Fish

No natural pond would be complete without its complement of fish. Apart from bringing life to the water, they help to control undesirable aquatic insect life such as mosquito and gnat larvae. While fish are desirable, it depends upon personal choice as to how many are introduced and of which species. Goldfish are extremely useful and resilient. So too are their fancy variety, the shubunkin, and the comet-tailed forms of each. Golden orfe and both golden and silver rudd are attractive fish which tend to shoal and live towards the surface of the pond. Tench are fish that live on the floor of the pond and are referred to as scavenging fish. They rarely show themselves, and although interesting characters, are of dubious decorative merit.

Before fish are introduced to a pool it is wise to disinfect them. Use a product based upon methylene blue and immerse them in it (see pages 192-3) before returning them to a small bag of water and floating this on the surface of the pond. After a short time, when the temperature of the water inside the bag has equalized with that in the pond, release them into the water.

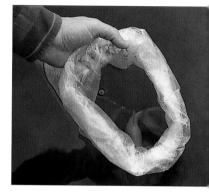

1 Prepare fish before introducing them to the pool by equalizing the water temperature in their bag with that in the pool. Roll down the top of the bag to make a collar.

STOCKING LEVELS

The guideline for the maximum stocking level of a pond is 2 cm (0.8 in) of fish per 50 liters (13.2 gallons) of water. So a pond holding 2000 liters (528 gallons) of water will support 80 cm of fish – four fish each 20 cm long or eight fish each 10 cm long, etc. However many fish the pond will theoretically hold, always understock to allow the fish to grow to the natural stocking level of the pond. Overcrowding results in poor growth and outbreaks of disease.

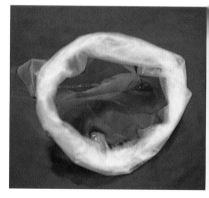

2 Float the bag containing some of the original water in which the fish were purchased on the surface of the pool. The temperatures will begin to equalize.

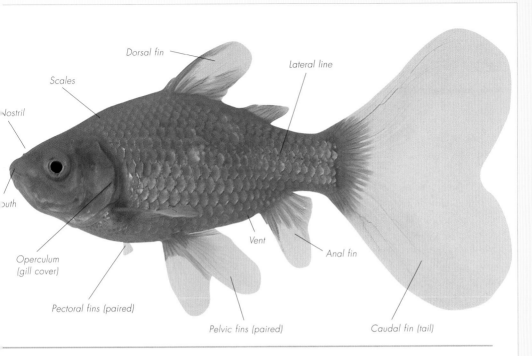

Dorsal fin

Scales

Nostril

Mouth

Operculum
(gill cover)

Pectoral fins (paired)

Pelvic fins (paired)

Lateral line

Vent

Anal fin

Caudal fin (tail)

3 Pour some pond water into the bag to assist with the temperature equalization process and to adjust the relative pH levels. Leave the bag for a further 20 minutes or so.

4 Once the temperature has equalized within the bag, the fish can be gently poured into the pool. For the first few days after introduction they may not be very visible.

PROJECT: Keeping Fish Healthy

Fish are an important component of most ponds. There is often a great urge to introduce them immediately after planting. This temptation should be resisted for at least a month so that the plants can settle down and the filter be given time to get established. If fish are introduced too early, they often disrupt the plants and cloud the water with disturbed compost.

When freshly purchased fish are introduced to a pond, it is prudent to disinfect them with an anti-fungal and anti-bacterial solution. This ensures that they do not bring infection to your pond. There are also various pond treatments that can be added to the water to prevent outbreaks of disease.

In a well-balanced pond there is no need to feed fish, but feeding is attractive for the gardener, for then the fish become tame and come to the surface when food is offered. There are many good foods around varying from flake and floating pellets to the more traditional biscuit meal and sinking pellets. Feed at the same point in the pool to encourage their prompt appearance and give no more food than they can clear up in 20 minutes. Any food left uneaten should be netted out, as decomposition of the residue will lead to the build-up of ammonia in the pond.

Above: *The beautiful iridescent colours of goldfish really help to bring a pool to life, particularly on a bright, sunlit day.*

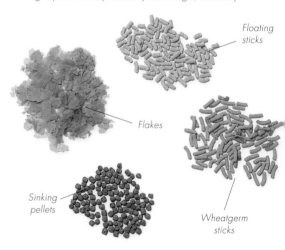

Floating sticks

Flakes

Sinking pellets

Wheatgerm sticks

Above: *There is a wide range of fish foods available to the pond keeper, all of which are scientifically produced. It is not really necessary to feed decorative fish in a well-balanced pond, but most water gardeners enjoy doing so.*

1 Add a protective disinfectant such as methylene blue to a bowl of water to create a bath.

2 Swim new fish in the bath for a minute as a precaution before introducing them to the pool.

3 There are various pond treatments that can improve water conditions and help to prevent disease outbreaks.

4 Mix in a bucket according to instructions; pour from the bucket into the pool and distribute freely in the water.

PROJECT: What Fish To Choose

Fish are important additions to the garden pond, adding movement, life, and color. They also control aquatic insect pests and mosquito larvae, so even for those gardeners who have little interest in fish keeping, they are valuable introductions.

In the well-planted garden pond, goldfish in their various varieties, along with the shubunkin variation, are the most useful type to choose. Goldfish are adaptable to a wide range of conditions, and in a favorable environment are likely to breed and produce a few young.

Golden orfe are surface-swimming shoaling fish, which have quite a high oxygen requirement. They are not suitable for very small ponds or warm summer climates, unless there is plenty of water movement from a fountain or waterfall to oxygenate the water. Green tench will live happily almost anywhere, as will a few colorful koi carp, although these can be quite destructive to submerged plant life unless introduced sparingly. And do remember that if you want to keep koi in quantity, they will need a special pond of their own with a dedicated filtration system.

Apart from ornamental fish, there are aquatic snails that have a role to play in the garden pond. The desirable kinds, like the ramshorn snail, graze on troublesome filamentous algae. All these have a flat shell and the general appearance of an ammonite. Spiral-shelled snails should be avoided, as these prefer to eat decorative plants.

FISH SELECTION

Black Moor
A black velvety variety of goldfish with bulbous eyes and a spreading fan-like tail.

Fantail
A red, or red-and-white variety of goldfish with a short rounded body and fan-like tail.

Goldfish
The common goldfish is excellent for the garden pond. It is available in red, gold, white, and combinations of those colors.

Golden Orfe
A slim, fast-swimming, shoaling fish. Pinkish or orange, often with a black marking on the head.

Shubunkin
A multicolored variety of goldfish in an array of rainbow colors, from red, orange and white, to grey and blue.

Green Tench
This dark, olive-green fish is usually introduced as a bottom-feeding scavenging fish.

Right: *A large water feature such as this can sustain quite a large population of fish. The rule of thumb to remember when calculating stocking levels is to allow 50 liters (13.2 gal) of water for every 2 cm (0.8 in) of fish.*

194

As well as the common goldfish, there are fancy varieties that can inhabit a garden pond.

Black Moor

Shubunkin

Goldfish

POND CARE AND MAINTENANCE

A well-established water feature with a natural ecological balance requires very little maintenance. However, there are a number of seasonal tasks that must be performed. Regular observation is also essential to ensure that all is well, for if the eco-system collapses, the pond will quickly become a disaster.

Water quality is important, but it should not become an obsession. Providing that there appears to be a natural balance, the water being clear or of an amber color with the fish swimming about contentedly, all is

well. There are test kits available for pH, nitrate and other aspects of water condition, but most are not needed while all is well. They are best used for establishing the cause of the problem if things start to go wrong.

Routine care for a water feature is much like that for any other part of the garden. As the blossoms of marginal plants start to fade,

Below: *The water garden takes on a different aspect in winter. It is important to make proper preparations over the winter months so that fish and plants get the best possible start when warmth returns in the spring.*

Tips & handy hints

In winter, prolonged icing over of a pond can cause distress for the fish, the noxious gases which result from the decomposition of detritus on the floor of the pool being trapped and sometimes causing asphyxiation. Replace the pump with an electric pond heater to maintain a small ice-free area, or else stand a pan of boiling water on the ice to melt through a hole for ventilation.

Never walk across a frozen pond, nor attempt to break the ice physically. Such activities are likely to concuss or kill the fish beneath.

When trimming back marginal aquatics, never cut hollow-stemmed kinds below water level. If these fill with water, they are liable to rot.

Left: *When the first frost arrives, the water garden should be prepared for the winter.*

deadhead them to prevent tiresome self-seeding. Do not worry about those of waterlilies or other deep-water aquatics; they fade away quite naturally. Remove faded foliage and thin excessive growth.

Regular division of all plants every two to three years is essential if they are to maintain their health and vigor. Between times feed them using a properly prepared aquatic fertilizer. In winter, some plants benefit from over-wintering buds or turions being taken indoors, and care needs to be taken to ensure that in cold weather vulnerable pond dwellers, especially the fish, are protected.

Understanding The Water Chemistry In The Pond

Understanding the chemistry of the pond is important if a good quality of water is to be maintained. If there is no overstocking of fish and plants are installed in numbers and varieties that ensure a natural balance, then there are few problems. However, it is as well to be aware of what can go wrong and why.

Problems mostly occur if the plant population goes into decline and fish population levels rise. This can have an adverse effect upon the nitrogen cycle (see diagram). It is the lack of control of nitrogenous wastes deriving from the fish that can lead to problems, especially a rise in ammonia levels.

Below: The Nitrogen Cycle – *this is how nitrogen circulates in a pond. The bacteria that convert one nitrogen-containing compound into another occur naturally. It is essential to encourage them to thrive in filters to prevent ammonia and nitrite building up.*

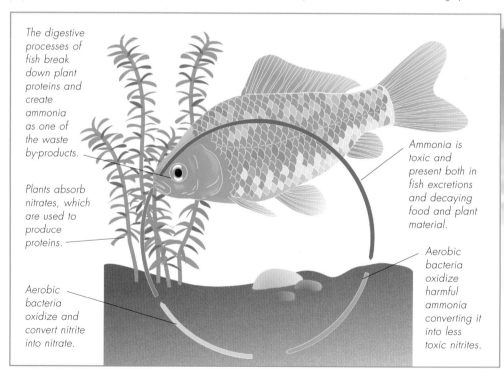

The digestive processes of fish break down plant proteins and create ammonia as one of the waste by-products.

Plants absorb nitrates, which are used to produce proteins.

Aerobic bacteria oxidize and convert nitrite into nitrate.

Ammonia is toxic and present both in fish excretions and decaying food and plant material.

Aerobic bacteria oxidize harmful ammonia converting it into less toxic nitrites.

Maintaining the Eco-Balance

Above: *Of all the troublesome algae, it is the filamentous kinds like blanket and flannelweed that cause the greatest distress. The simplest form of control is to remove it from the pond with a net or to twirl it round a stick and pull it out of the water in that way.*

1 Barley straw provides a solution to many algal problems by mopping up excess nutrients, which algae feed on, during decomposition. Barley straw decomposes very slowly. Take lengths of barley straw and bend and twist them into a ball.

2 Take a small square of garden netting and tie the screwed-up straw into a ball. The useful life of a barley straw ball is about four months during the summer.

3 Place the barley straw ball towards the edge of the pool and hide it discreetly. Attach a string to it so that once it starts to decompose, it can be easily retrieved and removed from the pool.

Understanding The Water Chemistry

In nature, nitrifying bacteria break down toxic wastes into less harmful products. This takes place as part of what is known as the nitrogen cycle. Organic material usually contains proteins in variable amounts. When protein is broken down either by bacterial decomposition or as a waste product of protein metabolism, ammonia is formed. Bacterial action converts ammonia, which is extremely toxic to fish, into less toxic nitrites. These in turn are converted into nitrates which are relatively harmless substances which are taken up as 'food' by plants and used in the construction of plant proteins. The process of converting ammonia into nitrate is called nitrification.

When there are considerable numbers of fish, the process of nitrification, which naturally occurs in the pond, will benefit from the action of a biological filter. Such a filter provides a home for beneficial bacteria to prosper. Even when the water chemistry of a pond appears to be healthy, it is wise to check periodically for nitrites. Most garden centers offer simple test kits which can be easily used by the gardener. They involve mixing a small sample of pond water with a chemical which then turns color and is compared with a test chart. There is a similar test which can determine the relative acidity or pH of the water. Although this is rarely as critical as for nitrite, it is useful to keep an eye on the acidity of the water.

While a natural balance of plants and sensible stocking level with fish is the most

Above: *An air pump dissipates oxygen through the water. This is helpful to fish and improves water quality.*

satisfactory method of maintaining stability, the introduction of physical, biological and UV filters can be recommended, depending upon circumstances. Using an air pump to improve the oxygen content of the water is also invaluable, especially where there is a heavy population of fish. These resemble aquarium pumps and they can improve water quality considerably, especially in the murky, often lifeless, bottom of the deeper pool.

1 The testing of pond water should be carried out routinely. It is essential to obtain a typical fresh sample in a small test tube.

2 For a pH test for water acidity a tablet is dissolved in the water sample. This colors the water, which is then matched against a chart.

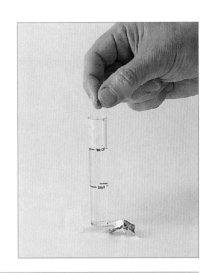

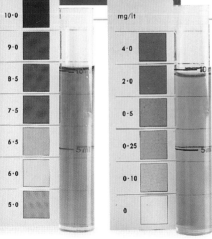

3 The results of most pond water tests are analyzed against a graduated color chart of comparative readings. The sample on the left shows a broad-range pH reading, while that on the right gives the result of a simple test for nitrite levels in the pond water.

ULTRA-VIOLET FILTER

Above: A UV filter is useful for the control of algae suspended in the water. The UV light kills algae as pond water flows through the filter.

Seasonal Care of a Water Feature

The eco-balance of a water feature, once established, has to be maintained. It is important to ensure that the balance of submerged subjects and both floating plants and the foliage of deep-water aquatics are controlled satisfactorily. Marginal plants, although of no great significance in maintaining a balanced eco-system, can disrupt it considerably if allowed to spread indiscriminately. So the regular lifting, division and trimming of plants is essential both during the spring and into the summer.

Leaves are also a great problem for pond owners. Natural ponds visually can tolerate a few more than most formal arrangements, but not when it comes to an accumulation causing problems. Irrespective of whether there are trees in your garden, leaves will find their way in during the autumn. They can blow in from neighboring gardens and always tend to swirl around and be pulled down onto the surface of the pond immediately when they come into contact with water.

Some leaves are extremely toxic, not to plants, but to fish and should be excluded by whatever means possible. These include those of the horse chestnut family (*Aesculus*), which are particularly noxious, as well as willows (*Salix*), which have properties similar to aspirin and can harm fish when they decompose in the pool. The temporary use of netting to protect the pool from fallen leaves is the best way of keeping them out.

During the winter it is important to winter-wash fruit trees of the plum and cherry (*Prunus*) family, for these are the over-wintering host of one of the most troublesome aquatic pests, the waterlily aphid. During the autumn, adult female aphids migrate to the trees and deposit eggs and die. These can be killed during the winter by spraying with tar oil wash, thus weakening their life cycle.

Above: *The occurrence of slime and algae cannot be wholly avoided, even in the best-balanced pools.*

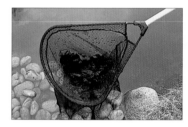

Above: *Fallen leaves are a nuisance in a pond, especially at autumn leaf fall. They should be netted out regularly.*

Above: *As winter approaches, it is important to remove dead or decaying foliage on marginal plants.*

Spring

- Aquatic plants can be planted.
- Lift and divide waterlilies and marginal plants as necessary.
- Take cuttings from submerged aquatics and replant where necessary.
- Sow the seeds of aquatic plants and bog garden subjects that are available from seed companies.
- Take stem cuttings of selected marginal aquatics. Increase waterlilies from eyes.
- Repot and replace the compost of any plants that require attention, but do not need dividing.
- If the pond requires cleaning out, the spring is the best time to do so.

Summer

- Control filamentous algae by twisting out with a stick.
- Introduce or replace any plants as required.
- Remove faded blossoms from marginal plants.
- Remove surplus carpeting floating plants with a net.
- Fertilize the compost of established waterlilies and marginals.
- Sow freshly collected seeds of aquatic plants.
- Cut back any excessive growth of aquatic plants.

Autumn

- Collect and store plantlets and turions of appropriate aquatics ready for the winter.
- Net the pool to keep out leaves.
- Cut back faded marginal plants, but do not cut hollow-stemmed aquatics below water level or else they might rot.
- Take root cuttings of bog garden plants like primulas.

Winter

- Ensure that an area of the surface is kept free from ice to permit the escape of noxious gases that may harm fish.

- Spray trees of the plum and cherry family with a winter wash (above) to kill off the over-wintering generation of waterlily aphids.

Index

Acknowledgements

The publisher would like to thank the following people and companies for their help with the preparation of this book: Anthony Archer-Wills and Gail Paterson at New Barn Aquatic Nurseries, West Chiltington; Mike and Wendy Yendell of Aristaquatics, Billingshurst; Old Barn Nurseries, Dial Post, Horsham; Graham and Howard Healey at Four Seasons Bonsai Nursery, East Peckham; Hillhout Ltd; Stephen Markham; Stuart Thraves at Blagdon, Bridgwater; Murrells Nursery, Pulborough; Graham Quick; Geoff Rogers; Stonescapes, Cranleigh; and Bulldog Tools.

Picture Credits

Unless otherwise credited below, the photographs in this book were taken by Neil Sutherland and are copyright © Interpet Publishing Ltd.

Eric Crichton Photos: front cover (Roger Platt), 1 (Erik de Maejer and Jane Hudson, RHS Chelsea 2002), 10bl (Country Living Garden, RHS Chelsea 1993), 13b (Amanda Broughton, RHS Hampton Court 2002), 18 (May and Watts, RHS Hampton Court 2003), 19t (Marney Hall, Iestyn Davies, Gill Hubson, RHS Hampton Court 2003), 34, 35t (Wyevale Garden Centre, RHS Chelsea 2001), 47 (Brian Tomes, RHS Hampton Court 2002), 60 (Alan Gardner, RHS Tatton Park 1999), 72bl, 80 (Janet Grant and Julian Tatlock, RHS Hampton Court 2003), 81b, 93 (J. Parker, RHS Tatton Park 2003), 105, 114-115, 116, 116-117, 120, 121t, 154-155 (Daniel Lloyd-Morgan, The Anglo-Aquarium Plant Co, RHS Hampton Court 2001), 157tl, 171tc, 171bl, 177bl, 177bc, 179tl, 179tc, 179tr, 179bl, 180, 181tl, 181tc, 181tr, 181bl, 183tr, 185bl, 187tc, 187bc, 187br, 188.

John Glover: 6 (Guy Farthing, RHS Hampton Court 2002), 11 (Charles Funke, RHS Chelsea 2002), 14-15 (Andy Sturgeon, RHS Chelsea 2001), 15 (Nathalie Charles, RHS Chelsea 2002), 36 (The Dower House), 46 (Julian Dowle, RHS Chelsea 2003), 61b, 73 (May and Watts, RHS Hampton Court 2002), 138, 157br, 172, 173bl, 173bc, 174, 175tl, 175bl, 175bc, 177tc, 177tr, 177br, 178, 181br, 182, 183tl, 183bc, 186, 187bl, 189tc, 189tr, 189bl, 196, 197.

Clive Nichols Garden Pictures: 2-3 (Paul Dyer, RHS Hampton Court 2001), 4 (Mark Walker, RHS Chelsea 2000), 8-9 (Shelia Stedman), 10tr (Erik de Maejer and Jane Hudson, RHS Chelsea 2003), 13t (Carolyn Hubble), 14 (Courseworks, RHS Hampton Court 2001), 16 (Privett Garden Products), 17 (Sarah Layton), 19b (Lisette Pleasance), 35b (Carole Vincent, Blue Circle, RHS Chelsea 2001), 61t (James Dyson and Jim Honey, Daily Telegraph, RHS Chelsea 2003), 72tr (Jean-Louis Cura, Marc Felix and Michele Schneider), 92 (Mark Laurence), 118 (The Gaudi Garden, RHS Hampton Court 2002), 119, 121b (Godstone Gardeners Club, RHS Chelsea 2000), 156, 170, 171tr, 176 (Lady Farm Somerset), 179br, 184 (Clare Matthews), 185bc, 187tl, 189tl, 189bc.

Plant Pictures World Wide (PPWW): 171bc, 171br, 173tl, 173tr, 173br, 175tc, 175tr, 175br, 177tl, 179bc, 181bc, 183tc, 183bl, 183br, 185tl, 185tc, 185br, 187tr, 189br.

Neil Sutherland Photolibrary: 12, 20-21, 58-59, 81t, 104.